LEADERS
IN
Heels

PASTOR PAUL CANNINGS, PH.D

Keynote
BOOKS

Leaders in Heels

ISBN-13: 978-1-963102-67-3 (Paperback)
ISBN-978-1-963102-66-6 (eBook)
ISBN-13: 978-1-963102-68-0 (Hardcover)

Published by Keynote Books

Bulk orders of this book may be obtained by contacting Defiance Press & Publishing, LLC.

Public Relations Dept. – Defiance Press & Publishing, LLC
281-581-9300

Defiance Press & Publishing, LLC
281-581-9300
info@defiancepress.com

Table of Contents

Introduction

Women in scripture may not have been kings, high priests, tribal leaders, Pharisees, or pastors, but they had a tremendous impact on Biblical history, accomplishing remarkable things for God. These women shaped future kings and warriors, impacted a nation entering the Promised Land, and were found virtuous in giving birth to the humanity of Jesus Christ. They were the first to show up at the tomb, prompting the disciples to go look for the risen Christ. They collaborated with their husbands to impact the Roman church. They discipled sons and grandsons to become influential pastors in the New Testament.

Eve may have shaped the view of women in the early parts of the Bible, but that view was reshaped and restored via Eunice and Lois, Timothy's mother and grandmother respectively, who helped train and prepare Timothy for his eventual discipleship with the Apostle Paul (2 Timothy 1:5; 2 Timothy 3:15). It was that kind of service Paul alluded to when he wrote, "But women will be preserved through the bearing of children if they continue in faith and love and sanctity with self-restraint" (1 Timothy 2:15). To some women in our present-day society, that verse may seem to diminish their potential, ambitions, and accomplishments. Additionally, perhaps for some women who cannot have children, the statement may seem to reduce their contribution to God's glory. That would be a misinterpretation, for such was not the Apostle Paul's intention.

I have been blessed by women who saw their roles as divine calls from God to further His kingdom for His glory. My mother, Anne Eleen Cannings, is one of those women. Each school-day, she taught eight kids their morning devotions. She faithfully did that after waking up early

5

to prepare lunch for her husband. At night, she would stop by our beds and encourage us to pray before going to sleep. She encouraged us to continue to learn the word of God on our own. When she found out I had accepted Christ, she sent me to Sister Clark who faithfully discipled me.

Sister Clark would come to the class even if it was raining—either walking or riding her bike. Most of the time, it was just me present in those classes with Sister Clark (my mother made sure I went each Sunday afternoon—no discussion). Sister Clark was always well prepared and was so patient in teaching me the scriptures. I kept thinking, hoping, that she would cancel class, but she was ever present, patiently explaining the Bible. I became a disciple of Christ at a young age because of Sister Clark's love, dedication, and care for me.

My mother's impact continued because she did a lot to get her family to America so that we could be educated in the United States. She sacrificed much for me to finish college, constantly telling me to persist until I received a doctorate degree. It was that constant influence on my spiritual growth and commitment to family and academics that has blessed me to serve the Lord in this present manner.

My mom and Sister Clark may not have pastored Living Word Fellowship Church from serving four couples to serving over four thousand members. They may not have directly developed the church and designed all its existing ministries. They did not design or build all the buildings, nor did they send missionaries to five countries in Africa and eleven islands in the Caribbean and Haiti where pastors, leaders, and their wives are being trained. My mom and Sister Clark are not directly touching lives through radio, television, the Internet, books, and articles. Neither are they connecting with sponsors through outreach programs for Living Word Fellowship Church...nonetheless, *they* made it all possible.

My mother also influenced the lives of her other children and grandchildren, including my sons, one of whom is my assistant pastor, a graduate of the Dallas Theological Seminary, and the first African-American dean for the Dallas Theological Seminary's Houston branch. My oldest son works with churches to build and develop schools and outreach buildings in Houston, Atlanta, and San Francisco. My older brother, John Cannings, has an after-school program that has reached hundreds of children in Nacogdoches, Texas over the years. Moreover, the ministries of her granddaughters, Priscilla Shirer and Chrystal Evans Hurst, have reached millions. In the same vein, I must mention their mom and my sister, Lois Evans, the late wife of Tony Evans, whose spiritual influence continues not only through her daughters but also her sons. And through all these relatives, my mom's influence remains strong.

My mom has passed on to be with the Lord after ninety-seven years of life. But has she? Did the passage listed above in 1 Timothy 2:15 restrict her potential, stifle her ambitions, and diminish her accomplishments? I beg to differ. One of the many roles to which God called my mother (aside from her spiritual gifts in service to her church and talents in working and leading people in the community) became her eternal blessing because she accepted God's design, worked within His structure, and remained faithful for His glory.

Whether leading from the home, leading from the church, or leading as community leaders, women have made great Biblical impact, leading to tremendous results for God's glory. This book examines women's commitment to God in the Old and New Testaments. It reviews and outlines how their respect for God's design and structure blessed God's progressive plan to impact the world, changing lives forever. As you read this book, I'd urge you to focus on the progressive development of their influence as outlined in the scriptures—instead of coming to any conclusions after reading just the introduction or any one chapter in the book.

Editor's comments:[1]

In the twenty-first century, the role of women in the Bible has been the subject of several books, sermons, podcasts, and social media posts. Dr. Paul Cannings' latest book, *Leaders in Heels*, sets the record straight on how women were foundational to the forward progress of the Kingdom of God in the Old and New Testaments. The time is now for Christendom to understand and accept the high value the Lord places on women who are completely surrendered to Him. This book is a must-read for all believers in Jesus Christ. Thus, it is our prayer that it is read with an open mind...and heart.

Mignette Y. Dorsey, D.Min.

Editor

1. Scriptural references are from the New American Standard Bible (NASB) or its updated edition (NASU), except where noted.

CHAPTER 1
Mary

The Transforming Power of Motherhood

Today, we live in a world that views motherhood as providing the best for one's children based on what the culture has to offer. The duties of a mother run the gamut from dressing kids up cute and getting their hair done just right to providing a comfortable home and the best that education has to offer. It also includes (but is not limited to) buying them video games and other technological trinkets, not to mention frenetic activities such as soccer, swimming, and tennis. Others believe their children will mature if placed in the best academic, social, or church environments.

What we are trying to do is put our children on the world's assembly line, hoping it yields impressive end-products. Yet, what sometimes emerge at the end of that assembly line are children who have no heart for God, who hate each other, and who have no morals. We have a generation that boasts of producing the best, yet we have the greatest crime rates, and much of that crime is committed by the youth. Add to that the increasing high school dropout rate and the increased number of sexual diseases in this generation. Something is wrong. We have yet to ask, "God, what is parenting that honors you?" We are yet to remember that "A wise son makes a father glad, but a foolish son is a grief to his mother" (Proverbs 10:1).

I find it amazing that when Mary was pregnant with Jesus, God did not tell Mary how to mother Him. Nowhere in the Bible did God give Mary instructions defining motherhood. He did not tell Mary, "Now that I have given you Jesus Christ, this is how you must raise Him." He just entrusted Mary and Joseph with His Son because of their commitment to do things God's way (Luke 1:38; Matthew 1:19, 24-25).

Mary was unique in that she was called to nurture and raise Christ. It was a decision God made without Mary's permission, yet the gift of a child is the same for any mother. "Behold, children are a gift of the Lord, the fruit of the womb is a reward" (Psalm 127:3). "But women will be preserved through the bearing of children if they continue in faith and love and sanctity with self-restraint" (1 Timothy 2:15). So, the only difference between Mary and any mother is that Mary's child was begotten by the Holy Spirit and is Christ.

To garner a more complete picture of Mary as a mother, we will examine the following passages: Luke 2:21-23, 39, Matthew 12:46, 13:53, and John 19:25-27. Indeed, what we glean from those passages are some of the most glorious aspects of mothering. The passages highlight three of Mary's character traits: 1) her commitment to God, 2) her persistence in keeping the family together, and 3) her faithful loyalty to Jesus from His birth to His death at Calvary.

Mary's Commitment to God

Mary had the most simplistic, quiet, and confidential way of taking on the greatest task she was given, and she was faithful in fulfilling what was required of her. She was a devout Jew, called upon by God to bear His Son, Jesus. Mary responded in fear at first but later willingly accepted the humiliation that she would encounter, finally understanding that people would view her calling as a glorious one (Luke 1:18-55).

In Luke 1:38, it is clear that Mary, who was age fourteen to sixteen at the time, was deeply committed to God. In verse 38, Mary says, "Behold, the Lord's bondservant; may it be done to me according to your word." She says that after she stops being afraid and after understanding that she was going to be embarrassed and humiliated by having a baby out of wedlock. The word "bondservant" indicates that Mary was committed to God to the point of death. It also suggests Mary was saying she would serve God at the level of a slave for life.

In other words, she was not looking for any payment or reward. She was not expecting God to make her rich, popular, or great for having His son. Indeed, her social status did not change. Mary was just glad to be God's slave as she served God's agenda. Eve said something similar after giving birth to Cain: "Now the man had relations with his wife Eve and she conceived and gave birth to Cain, and she said, 'I have gotten a manchild with the help of the Lord'" (Genesis 4:1).

Mary understood Jewish law. She knew that being pregnant out of wedlock could mean that she would not be allowed to marry Joseph and even risk being stoned to death. She could have also been cast aside by her family since her pregnancy suggested she had been unfaithful to Joseph, her betrothed. Such a scenario surely created humiliation for her family (and this may have happened since we never hear anything to the contrary from Mary's mother and father). Despite all, Mary was committed to God to be the mother of His Son, no matter the cost. She was all in.

Another trait Mary possessed was humility. In Matthew 1, her humility drove her faithfulness. Matthew 1:18 says, "When His mother Mary had been betrothed to Joseph, before they came together, she was found to be pregnant by the Holy Spirit." According to Matthew 1:19, Joseph discovered that Mary was already three months pregnant. Think of the embarrassment, the humiliation! I don't know anyone who would jump up and say, "Praise the Lord!" in such a situation. Yet, Mary told Joseph what took place and did not make any demands. God had decided to make her pregnant, and she was focused. Again, one never hears a word about Mary's parents being involved in any of this. It did not matter to Mary since this was God's plan for her life. A true bondslave.

Many mothers have had their children outside of marriage. Lots of promises were initially made, but in the end, the mother was left with all the responsibility. We must remember that every child is a gift from God—not some, but every child (Psalm 127:3). I know such a predicament can be humiliating, but it is definitely not the end. Even Mary was also a single mother for a certain period (remember the passage I provided earlier in 1 Timothy 2:15).

Despite the humiliation these circumstances must have imposed on both Joseph and Mary and despite all the adjustments they had to make, their faithfulness to God produced positive results for their entire family. In this way, raising children is first allowing the Lord to grow us. Subsequently, his spiritual influence, which is evident in our commitment to discipleship, so shapes our character that our children see more of Christ in us. The children see "Christ and the church" (Ephesians 5:23-24) operating in their home. This allows the Holy Spirit to shape not just us but our children. They are nurtured by the fruit of the Spirit they see radiating through us (Galatians 5:22-25)—and not by the flesh that leads to unresolved arguments, selfish decisions, abusive language, and sometimes, unfortunately, divorce, which in turn creates angry children.

Now, consider Hagar. She did not ask Abraham and Sarah to make her a surrogate mother. Nowhere in the scriptures did it say that she fell in love with Abraham and wanted to be with him. Abraham and Sarah made the decision, and Hagar had no choice in the matter. Despite her circumstances, God allowed Hagar to become pregnant. Further, Hagar did not ask Ishmael to bully Isaac. He was the older brother, and that is what older brothers do sometimes. Moreover, it was God who allowed Abraham to release Hagar. By putting only bread and water on her shoulders, Abraham made it clear that was all the child support she was going to get (Genesis 21:14).

Hagar found herself alone in the wilderness (Genesis 21:1-20). She could not go home to her parents. She had a mixed-race child by a sheep herder. Yet, Hagar loved her son, "for she said, 'Do not let me see the boy die'" (Genesis 21:16). God was faithful. "What is the matter with you, Hagar? Do not fear, for God has heard the voice of the lad where he is" (Genesis 21:17-18). With the Lord's help, Hagar faithfully and humbly raised her child, and he became a leader of a nation, lived a long life (Genesis 25:17), and came back and buried his father (Genesis 25:9). Furthermore, it was the Ishmaelites who rescued Joseph from the well and took him to Egypt.

As I was sitting in my study one day, my wife and one of my sisters were having a chat in the room. My sister stood there for a minute, looked at me and my wife, and said,

> The reason I love my mother is that mothering became her life, it became everything— her person, her character, her thinking, her focus, her daily living. Nothing ever took its place, and the reason I'm so dedicated to my mother is because there is nobody in this world who could have done for me what she has done. Even when I became pregnant outside of marriage, everyone denied me but my mother. There is nobody that could ever take her place in my life.

It is not what goes wrong that should guide our decisions. It is God's promises and our willingness to trust Him that should direct us so that the past remains the past as God shapes a greater future.

"And we know that God causes all things to work together for good to those who love God, to those who are called according to *His* purpose" (Romans 8:28). Please do not forget the most important words—"those who love God"—because "those who love God" keep His commandments (John 14:15).

The world is the world. It is evil, run by Satan (1 John 5:19). Satan is not friendly; he just appears that way, like bait on a hook (John 10:10). So, life is not always going to be fair. "Beloved, do not be surprised at the fiery ordeal among you, which comes upon you for your testing, as though some strange things were happening to you" (1 Peter 4:12). The question then is this: What will we do when life does not work the way we want it to? Are we going to keep the faith (which is the only fight we have as per 1 Timothy 6:12)? Or are we going to allow the circumstances to control our response instead of taking our directions from Christ? When we, like Mary, decide to allow God to direct us, it does not mean life is easy. It simply means that the results are better, and His yoke turns out to be easier to bear (Matthew 11:28-30).

Mary's Dedication to Family

Mary remained focused because of the word of God. I am sure that her commitment to the Word influenced how her husband executed what the law required of them in raising Jesus. In Luke 2:21-22 and 39, Joseph and Mary obeyed the law, circumcising Christ on the eighth day. They also obeyed the Word of God in naming Him Jesus, exactly as God had instructed by way of the angel.

Mary performed the purification rituals after forty days and went down to the temple, presenting her offering, "A pair of turtledoves and two pigeons," in complete obedience to the law (Luke 2:22-24). These verses in Luke 2 refer to Exodus 13:2 and 12, and Leviticus

12:8. Jesus's parents fulfilled the laws of Moses properly and piously. The particular sacrifice they offered indicates that they were poor as explained in Leviticus 12:8. (Recall David said in Psalm 37:25 that he "had not seen the righteous forsaken or his descendants begging for bread.") Following the custom, Mary would lay hands on the pigeons before a priest would take them to the southwest corner of the altar, wringing one bird's neck as a sin offering and burning the other as a burnt offering.

Though it was a three-day walk to the temple, they arrived at the exact time the law required because God told her when to go and what to do, and she did exactly as He said. She was so faithful to the Word that she did whatever the Word said. Her faithfulness was not dependent on circumstances but on her commitment to God as a bondslave.

It is important to note that faithfulness to God produces results that the world can never provide. It even impacts unbelieving family members: "For the unbelieving husband is sanctified through his wife, and the unbelieving wife is sanctified through her believing husband; for otherwise your children are unclean, but now they are holy" (1 Corinthians 7:14). So, what matters most is that a couple is faithful to what God has called them to do. This faithfulness not only blesses them in heaven but also on earth. Think of passages such as Psalm 112 or 128. "Unless the Lord builds the house, they labor in vain who build it; unless the Lord guards the city, the watchman keeps awake in vain. It is vain for you to rise up early, to retire late, to eat the bread of painful labors; for He gives to His beloved even in his sleep" (Psalm 127:1-2).

To comply with the law, Mary and Joseph took Jesus, then aged twelve, to the temple in Jerusalem for the Feast of the Passover:

The age of twelve would have been one year before Jesus officially became an adult Israelite and accepted responsibility for fulfilling the law (its analogy to Roman coming-of-age rituals supports other evidence for an official entrance to adulthood around this age).[2] At age 12, every Jewish boy was called 'a son of the law,' being then put under a course of instruction and trained in fasting and attendance of public worship, besides learning a trade.[3]

Families usually traveled long distances in caravans, which afforded protection from robbers, who were commonly encountered on pilgrimages to Jerusalem. Traveling with a caravan in which neighbors from their town would watch the community children together, Mary and Joseph might have assumed that the near-adult Jesus was with companions, especially if by now they had younger children with them. If we assume a pace of twenty miles per day (though perhaps slower, depending on transportation and the children), Nazareth would be a little over a three-day journey along the shortest route.

Luke 2:41-52 states that after traveling for a full day from Jerusalem to Nazareth, Joseph and Mary noticed Jesus was not with them in the caravan. After feverishly looking everywhere for Him, Mary's passion prompted her to leave the caravan (where she and Joseph were safe) and return to Jerusalem. This probably meant the rest of the children had to return with them. Can you imagine how mad Jesus's siblings were? Perhaps they were thinking, "She never spanks Jesus, and she always thinks that He is right." Add to that the fact that they had spent another three days in Jerusalem looking for Him before finally discovering Him engaged in discourse with teachers in the temple.

Some teachers during that period reportedly conducted their classes in the temple courts; the famous Hillel and Shammai may have been

2. Alfred Edersheim, *The Life and Times of Jesus the Messiah.* (New York: Herrick, 1886). (Des Moines, WA: Biblesoft, Inc., 2015).

3. Robert Jamieson, Andrew Robert Fausset, and David Brown, *Jamieson, Fausset, and Brown Commentary on the Whole Bible* (Grand Rapids: Zondervan, 1961). (Des Moines, WA: Biblesoft, Inc., 2015).

two such teachers. Asking questions was used both in teaching and in learning, but it was important for learners to ask intelligent questions, as Jesus did. One scholar argues that Mary and Joseph must have set out for home before the close of the feast:

> We read in the Talmud that the members of the Temple-Sanhedrin, who, on ordinary days, sat as a court of appeal from the close of the morning to the time of the evening sacrifice, were wont, upon Sabbaths and feast-days, to come out upon the terrace of the temple, and there to teach. In such popular instruction the utmost latitude of questioning would be given. It is in this audience, which sat upon the ground, surrounding, and mingling with the doctors, and hence, during, not after, the feast, that we must seek the child Jesus.[4]

Despite the fact that all who heard Jesus speak "were amazed at His understanding and His answers," Mary still had words for him: "Son, why have You treated us this way? Behold, your father and I have been anxiously looking for You!" (Luke 2:47-49). It should be noted that fidelity to and respect for one's family was so heavily emphasized in that culture that such words must have struck their hearers quite forcefully. Many Jewish interpreters regarded the command to honor one's father and mother as the most important of laws. Thus, Jesus "…went down with them and came to Nazareth, and He continued in subjection to them; and His mother treasured all these things in her heart" (Luke 2:51).

It would appear that at some point after this incident and before the crucifixion, Joseph died, leaving Mary a single parent and widow (most men died at the age of about forty-five in those times). Nevertheless, Mary worked to keep her family together, continually demonstrating her dedication to obey God in all matters related to Jesus and the

---

4. Edersheim, *The Life and Times of Jesus,* 247. (Des Moines, WA: Biblesoft, Inc., 2015).

family. Indeed, Mary's concern for Jesus continued into his adulthood.

You may be thinking that raising Jesus had to be easy because He was fully God and fully man. I beg to differ. Do you know how complicated that was? How would you like the task of raising the God-Man? How would you like to have the task of raising a child who knew more than you (Luke 2:52)? And even though Mary believed in her son as the Messiah, Jesus's half-siblings did not, so the blended family was divided (Acts 1:14; John 7:5). Can you imagine some of the tension that might have colored their interactions? For instance, one of her children could have said, "How come you never discipline Jesus?" Still, Mary's dedication to her family was demonstrated by the way she kept them together. She did this knowing that her son would soon be her Savior (Matthew 27:55-56; Luke 2:19, 34-35, and 51) even though the rest of her children did not understand (1 Corinthians 15:7).

In Mark 3:20, Jesus comes back home a super star. Everybody knows about His powers, His miracles, and His teachings. People crowd around Him. Yet some recognize Him as merely the carpenter's son from a poor family (Luke 4:22). They knew Him from the time he was a young boy in their village. In those days, most villages were small, and most people knew one another. Some may have even been part of the caravans that traveled to and from the temple for Passover. So, here was Jesus, coming back home as somebody special (or so they might have surmised), which made them despise Him (Matthew 13:57). Mary was thrown into the midst of this conflict because of her love for her son.

Overall, the crowd that had gathered in Jesus's hometown was a hostile one. According to Mark 3:20-35, the crowd did not believe in Jesus, saying he was of Satan. They were pressing in on Jesus, so much so that He could not even get away to get something to eat. Soon, Mary and several of her other sons (Jesus' half-brothers) arrived. The scripture says, "…when His own people heard about this, they came out to take custody of Him; for they were saying, 'He has lost His senses'"(Mark 3:21).

The crowd, no doubt, wanted to remove Him from the village, but they could not find a good reason. Thus, the urgency for Him to respond to His family's call: "Behold, Your mother and Your brothers are standing outside seeking to speak to You" (Matthew 12:46-50; Mark 3:31-32). Mary and her sons were trying to rescue Jesus. Mary was most likely glad her Son had returned home, and she was trying to take charge, just like at the wedding feast (John 2:1-6).

Remember, at the wedding feast, Jesus Christ was with His disciples when Mary told Him to make more wine. Jesus Christ addressed her as "Woman"—in other words "Ma'am" or "Madam" in their culture. Jesus was telling Mary, His earthly mother, that she could not decide when His ministry should begin. When she exercised her authority as it related to His ministry, she was "Madam."

For the same reason, Jesus said to the crowd that had informed Him of his family's arrival, "Who is My mother and who are My brothers?" And stretching out His hand toward His disciples, He said, "Behold My mother and My brothers! For whoever does the will of My Father who is in heaven, he is My brother and sister and mother" (Matthew 12:48-50; Mark 3:31-35). I wonder how these words would have resonated with Mary.

Thinking of one's co-religionists as brothers and sisters was common. Respecting older people as mothers and fathers was also widespread, but allowing the ties in the religious community to take precedence over one's family ties was unheard of in Judaism. It was as though He regarded his new family as more important than his natural one. (Like other Jewish teachers, Jesus commonly employed hyperbole, or rhetorical exaggeration.)

However, He was not rejecting his earthly family altogether. He was simply stating his priorities because they wanted to declare him mentally incompetent and rescue Him from the dangers He was sure to face from religious authorities if He continued on that path (Mark 3:21).

Jesus did not allow Mary or His brothers to take over. He remained focused on His mission, but Mary refused to do nothing on seeing her son in danger. Again, it appears that Joseph had passed on by that time, so it was obvious that Mary was doing what she perceived as her job, which was taking care of her family. Her sons followed her and were ready to take Jesus home, just as Mary had instructed. Remember that all of this was done in the midst of scribes accusing Him, crowds pressing Him so hard He could not eat, and Jesus confronting and challenging them for making false accusations.

Mary had to manage all of that as a single woman as she saw the tension simmering in not just her own home, but also in all those who sought to kill her first-born son. Mary accepted her call, remaining faithful no matter how humiliating the circumstances. She faithfully executed her responsibilities—as did my mother in raising me and my siblings.

I remember growing up and being involved with my mom's early-morning devotions. Every morning at six, my mother put the Word into our minds. Every morning, eight children sat on the bed in the girls' bedroom. (Our house only had three bedrooms: one for our parents and one each for the four girls and the four boys). Her husband arose at five to catch a train for work, and she packed his bag for lunch. Yet, she still woke up eight kids and trained them in the Word of God. And she would always say, "There is nothing in life. Nobody owes you nothing, and nobody has to do anything for you. Your job in life is to stick with the Word."

I never forgot that in college. Though for the first time I could do what I wanted, I somehow found myself not wanting to miss my devotion time because my mother, for all those years, had made sure I had my personal devotions. Every night, she would make sure to remove my comic books (no matter how well I thought I had hidden them) and teach me how to conduct personal devotion at night. She also made sure I was exposed to biblical teaching outside the home.

There was a program for kids aged twelve called Inquirers Class. "You're going to it," my mom said. She never asked me if I wanted to go; she simply said, "Son, you are twelve. It's time to go to Inquirers Class." And then she would get up and walk me to church. Similarly, Mary probably said, "Jesus, you ready? We're going to the feast." That is faithfulness. Parents today might ask their kids whether they want to go to church, the same children whom David describes as "born in sin and shaped in iniquity" (Psalm 51:5). We are not just providers. The school does not supervise character development or teach how to be a good father or mother. The world is run by Satan (1 John 5:19). There is no way the world's assembly line can produce men and women of character, much less of godly character.

Our school was no more than a ten-minute walk from our house, and I would run home after playing soccer because my mother's food was better than the cafeteria fare. I had no problems eating. I'll never forget coming up the backsteps for lunch and hearing my mom praying to God for me. It changed my life. She did not remember that prayer she had uttered out loud.

"God, I don't know about this one, Paul. I whip him. I go to the schoolhouse after him, but he just loves to play. God, will you get this boy to be serious about you?" Short but succinct, that prayer had stopped me on the backsteps.

The world always tries to make us self-sufficient and proud. It teaches us, especially if we are educated, that our achievements are what define us and our families. The world projects that philosophy, and people make a lot of money following that maxim. Yet, God says that in order to avoid conforming to the ways of the world, we must renew the mind so that the world's way of thinking does not influence us (Romans 12:2).

The world does not want God's structure to be our passion. Only God can raise His own creation. I do not care about how sophisticated you are, nor about the level of education you may have attained. No college class can teach a woman how to be a mother. No class in junior high or high school teaches a woman how to be a mother. The best person to shape a character is Christ through the ministry of the Holy Spirit. Timothy became a great man of God because of his mother and grandmother, who allowed God to shape their and Timothy's lives, despite him having an unsaved father (2 Timothy 1:5; 3:15). In other words, his mother's spiritual influence sanctified the home (1 Corinthians 7:14).

Ladies, you cannot raise a child when you cannot see around the corner; you cannot raise a child when you cannot see the child's future. We must give ourselves to God so that our example leads our children to Christ. One day, my son asked me, "Daddy, what do you want me to be?" I replied as follows:

What I want you to become has nothing to do with your degree. It is irrelevant. What I want you to be is a man who would love your wife. I want you to be the man who would raise your children. What I want you to be is a good provider. What I want you to be is a man of morals, and the only way to learn that while you are single is to commit to grow in Christ so that He can shape your life, through the ministry of the Holy Spirit, to become like Christ.

It is being like Christ that makes a marriage (Ephesians 5:25 and 32). I also told my son that I wanted him to be a person who respects his parents in order to learn what it takes to have a child respect him. When young people grow up to develop Christ-like character, homes are more peaceful and stable, politicians are humbler and more upright, and the executives of companies are more efficient. That is what impacts the health of our communities, cities, states, and countries.

Creating a peaceful home requires faithfulness to His Word, a complete commitment to surrender to it by trusting Him, and a dedication to making our families work, regardless of how far it stretches us. No matter how much education we have, the world cannot teach us how to parent so that we cultivate wholesome characteristics in our children. The only person who can shape a life is Christ because He *is* life and came to give us abundant life and to establish a friendship with us (John 10:10; 15:13). This is why I truly believe that the best way to raise a child is to first allow Christ to mature us for His glory and blessing. Once we are committed to do so, our children can become disciples because we can teach them to observe what God is commanding them to do (Matthew 28:19-20). We must allow Christ to define and redefine us so that the world does not shape our identities or our purpose.

Mary: Faithfully Loyal to the End

The crucifixion of Jesus was a dangerous time. Yet, imagine Mary who was present at the fateful spot, in the midst of darkness and of vicious soldiers nailing Christ to the cross, dead people coming back to life, and an earthquake, to top it off! Still, she stood there without her other sons present beside her. Mary, the mother of Jesus Christ's humanity, faithfully served God and sincerely believed that her Son was the true Messiah. Jesus was born of the Holy Spirit, but He was still her son, and therefore a member of her family. Mary was determined to take care of him, to remain loyal to her Son even to the point of His death (John 19:25-27). She never left his side.

In the past, dying fathers often exhorted sons to take care of surviving mothers (which they normally would do). So, a primary responsibility in Jewish custom, which included honoring one's father and mother, was providing for them in their old age (1 Sam. 22:3). Jesus's mother was probably a widow in her mid- to late-forties and lived in a society where women rarely earned much income. She was therefore especially dependent on her eldest son for support. Jesus, being the oldest in the family, did not want to leave His mother unattended. He knew the love John had for Him, so He trusted the man who stayed with Him to help His mother (John 19:25-27).

Jesus honored Mary at the cross, not because of her education or status in society. He honored her because of her faithfulness in obeying God and her love for her family. Even though Jesus was fully man and fully God, He remembered his faithful mother at the cross and made sure she and his brothers were included in the New Testament church in Acts 1:14. None of Jesus's half-siblings believed He was the Christ at this time, but they did believe in Him after His death, burial, and resurrection, according to John 7:5, I Corinthians 15:7, Acts 1:14, and Acts 15:13.

Mary stayed on the course all the way to the cross. Her humility allowed her to never become too embarrassed to follow, never become too much of a mother to accept her son as her Savior, and never become too proud to allow her nephew to care for her as Christ so ordered. She became a great woman because she found ways to release herself to the will of God. Her complete dependence on God demonstrated her humility.

In Mary's day, she was poor and of no acclaim in the eyes of the world. She did not gain any considerable societal status. However, eternally, she will be great in the kingdom of God. Likewise, in the eyes of the world, the Laodiceans were viewed as rich and achieving much, but in God's eyes, they were "wretched and miserable, and poor and blind and naked" (Revelation 3:17).

Even though Mary was faced with the task of raising the God-Man, she did it faithfully and with dignity. This process caused her to be blessed. Perhaps these lines from the scriptures best summarize Mary, the mother of our Lord's humanity: "For whoever wishes to save his life shall lose it, but whoever loses his life for My sake, he is the one who will save it. For what is a man profited if he gains the whole world, and loses or forfeits himself?" (Luke 9:24-26).

Also, let's consider the following excerpt:

Truly, truly, I say to you, unless a grain of wheat falls into the earth and dies, it remains by itself alone; but if it dies, it bears much fruit. He who loves his life loses it; and he who hates his life in this world shall keep it to life eternal. If anyone serves Me, let him follow Me; and where I am, there shall My servant also be; if anyone serves Me, the Father will honor him (John 12:23-26).

It is not about who a person may be when the call to be a mother is presented to them (Psalm 127:3); it is more about how they allow the Lord to use them that makes them great (Proverbs 31:28). No mother knows who they have birthed until the child grows up. So how they raise the child is everything because the child can become great but still lack character. The child can become a person of significance but have no heart for God. "A wise son makes a father glad, but a foolish man despises his mother" (Proverbs 15:20). It is difficult to start as a child that is born in sin, shaped in iniquity (Psalm 51:5), and has foolishness in their hearts (Proverbs 22:15) and then go on to become a person of great character, but it is this process that, in God's opinion, provides eternal blessings to a mother: "But women shall be preserved through the bearing of children if they continue in faith and love and sanctity with self-restraint" (1 Timothy 2:15). After Solomon made many descriptive remarks about the woman from Proverbs 31, he ends the chapter in this manner: "Her children rise up and bless her; Her husband also, and he praises her, saying: Many daughters have done nobly, but you excel them all. Charm is deceitful and beauty is vain, but a woman who fears the Lord, she shall be praised" (Proverbs 31:29-30).

CHAPTER 2
Bathsheba & Abigail

From Pain to Promise

The story of Bathsheba is powerful because it teaches us about a woman who went through a horrible experience of being sexually abused, widowed, and bereft of her first child. Still, she raised a son (in all probability single-handedly) who became the renowned King Solomon whom God blessed with vast wisdom and who later wrote three Old Testament books (Proverbs, Ecclesiastes, and the Song of Solomon).

Bathsheba went from being sexually abused to sitting on a throne near her son, Solomon, who loved her so much he kept her close to himself. One admires this woman because instead of allowing horrific circumstances to define her, Bathsheba remained humble and focused, which empowered her to become the refined woman of Proverbs 31.

Some might question whether Bathsheba was sexually abused when she ended up marrying King David. I, for one, consider it sexual abuse when soldiers assigned to protect the king come to your home and force you to return to the king in order to be intimate with him. Nevertheless, some commentators dare assert that Bathsheba played a role in this:

Although David is held responsible for the sin, Bathsheba was not without blame. She came at his request, seemingly without hesitation, and offered no resistance to his desires (at least as far as the record is concerned). The fact that she was bathing in the uncovered court of a house in the heart of a city, into which anyone could look down from the roofs of neighboring houses or from higher ground, does not say much for her modesty, even if she had no ulterior motive, as some commentators suggest. However, this does not excuse David from the enormity of his transgression against the Lord's statutes and against one of his top fighting men.[5]

I strongly disagree with that position. One of the reasons for doing so is that the scriptures say this after David slept with Bathsheba: "and when she had purified herself from her uncleanness, she returned to her house" (2 Samuel 11:4). The scripture does not say she returned to David. It says that she perceived herself as unclean and so purified herself; this also means she knew about the Levitical Law and was obedient to it. In fact, Bathsheba's response to what transpired shows that she considered the act with King David sinful. On the other hand, there is no passage that says David went to the temple, purified himself, and confessed his sin. To the contrary, David committed additional misdeeds to cover up his sin.

For instance, when Bathsheba discovered she was pregnant, she informed David who tried to conceal the pregnancy. That ploy ended with Uriah, her husband, getting killed on the battlefield at David's behest. Bathsheba was then thrust into a whirlwind of life-changing circumstances—all because of David's lust. And to think that Uriah, a loyal warrior, was literally fighting for the man who had sexually abused his wife!

It is really a horrific story of a woman who, within days, went from minding her own business and anxiously waiting for Uriah to sleeping

---

5. C. F. Pfeiffer, *The Wycliffe Bible Commentary: Old Testament.* (Chicago: Moody Press, 1962). (Des Moines, WA: Biblesoft, Inc., 2015).

with David simply because she was beautiful, and he desired to have her (2 Samuel 11:6-13; 2 Samuel 11:2). It is not like David did not know the scriptures. For David himself wrote in Psalm 119:11, "Thy word I have treasured in my heart, that I may not sin against Thee." David therefore knew the Bible taught that a man must not covet another man's wife or uncover her nakedness (Exodus 20:13-17; Leviticus 18). Further, in his commentary, John Walton explains the extent of his deceit for it seems David knew who Bathsheba was all along:

> The father of Bathsheba is Eliam, a member of David's special cadre of 'mighty men' (2 Sam. 23:34) and therefore the head of an influential household. This Eliam is the son of Ahithophel, one David's most respected advisors (2 Sam. 15:12; 16:23). This information, along with the fact that her husband, Uriah the Hittite, is also one of the 'mighty men' (2 Sam. 23:39), suggests that David knew exactly whose house he was looking at and was well acquainted with Bathsheba (an alternative translation suggest that it was David who said, "Is this not Bathsheba?")[6]

One probably wonders how Bathsheba survived seemingly without a support system. For we do not read about anyone who nurtured her after the death of Bathsheba's first child, nor do we learn that David was so in love with her that he spent significant time raising Solomon with his wife. Instead, after David made her his wife, Bathsheba became a part of the harem, and probably functioned like most single parents raising a child. Her only advantage was the provisions from the king.

Bathsheba seems to have been a woman who feared the Lord. She listened to God when she purified herself (even though she was not at fault for the assault). When she became pregnant, she did not seek an

---

6. Victor Harold Matthews, Mark W. Chavalas, and John H Walton, *The IVP Bible Background Commentary: Old Testament* (Downers Grove, IL: InterVarsity Press, 2000). (Des Moines, WA: Biblesoft, Inc., 2015).

abortion but informed David, who married her after having her husband killed. Then after the baby died, she endured being comforted by her abuser (2 Samuel 12:24). Still, Bathsheba submitted to David, and God blessed them with another child, Solomon. She probably knew that God was clear in expecting that nobody would touch His anointed one (1 Samuel 26:11).

Nowhere do we find Bathsheba bitter or resentful towards David or God, despite the fact that she received no explanation from God as to why her life had changed so drastically. She accepted whatever the Lord planned for her to encounter and lived out a life surrendered to God. She had no power to change anything, like whether her first child lived or died. At every juncture, Bathsheba was found faithful, be it as a wife waiting on her husband to return from war, as a widow forced to accept her abuser as her new husband, as a mother whose child died, or as a woman who was comforted by her abuser. After all these mishaps, Bathsheba was found to be faithful enough to raise a king.

How many women would have been destroyed by such events, upset at God, and determined to find a way to make a man's life miserable while bitterly raising a child? Bathsheba was not that kind of person. She seems to have lived a quiet life until the prophet Nathan told her that another one of David's sons, Adonijah, was secretly trying to usurp David's throne, a throne David had promised to Solomon. Bathsheba had reason to be concerned about Adonijah's revolt. Theologian John Walvoord explains that "Customarily in the ancient Near East a new monarch would purge his political enemies when he came to power, as Solomon did later" (I Kings 2:13-46).[7]

Bathsheba was a humble woman who listened to God. When it was

---

7. J. F. Walvoord, R. B. Zuck, and the Dallas Theological Seminary. *The Bible Knowledge Commentary: An Exposition of the Scriptures* (1:488). (Wheaton, IL: Victor Books, 1983-c1985). (Des Moines, WA: Biblesoft, Inc., 2015).

time to establish her son as king, she responded in obedience to God's direction. Having received counsel from Nathan, she humbly did as Nathan instructed, for David had vowed that Solomon would be king. The scripture says that when she came into David's presence, she was focused. The verb "came" denotes that she did not intend to stop her progressive action until the task was done. In other words, she came with purpose and did not plan to stop until she had accomplished what she was instructed to do: secure Solomon's future as king. In accepting Nathan's advice, she behaved in a surprising way. First Kings 1:16-21 says that she "bowed and prostrated herself before the king, and the king said, 'What do you wish?'"

It is hard to imagine how, with all she had endured, she could still prostrate before the king. She could have stood erect and unyielding. After all, she was the queen. Moreover, it might have been a very emotionally charged encounter for Bathsheba considering that during her audience with David, he was lying next to a young girl, Abishag, who was keeping him warm. (Note that David did not have relations with Abishag; she was merely keeping him warm. As there were no heaters in the palace, it could mean that they were wearing very little clothing, were lying very close together in bed, or were even lying together naked.) Still, Bathsheba bowed before her husband. After David assured Bathsheba that Solomon would be king, she prostrated before him again. Walvoord explains her actions as follows:

> With gratitude for his granting her request Bathsheba bowed before her king. The expression, May my lord the king…live forever (cf. v. 31), is a common expression found often in Scripture signifying a desire that God would bless a monarch by granting him long life. It is a complimentary wish; God had promised to bless the righteous with

length of days. These words therefore implied that the king had acted righteously and was worthy of God's blessing.[8]

Bathsheba could have grabbed this chance to exact payback, as David was frail and vulnerable at that moment. But no, she bowed, as if to say, "You are still my King. You may be my husband, but you are my King, and I prostrate myself. I am in total submission to you because you, the anointed King, is my husband." Furthermore, Bathsheba did not have to fight for her son to be crowned king because God kept David alive long enough to ensure Solomon's coronation in a publicly and powerfully legislated process, which was orchestrated by David himself (1 Kings 1:38-53).

Bathsheba's efforts seemed to pay off, for nowhere do we see David teaching and helping the older Solomon until it was time for the latter to ascend to the throne:

> As David's time to die drew near, he charged Solomon his son, say-ing, 'I am going the way of all the earth. Be strong, therefore, and show yourself a man. And keep the charge of the Lord your God, to walk in His ways, to keep His statutes, His commandments, His ordinances, and His testimonies, according to what is written in the law of Moses, that you may succeed in all that you do and wherever you turn, so that the Lord may carry out His promise which He spoke concerning me, saying, 'If your sons are careful of their way, to walk before Me in truth with all their heart and with all their soul, you shall not lack a man on the throne of Israel' (1 Kings 2:1-5).

For his part, Solomon listened to and obeyed his father, and God blessed him (I Kings 3:5-14). Though his throne was fully established (not just by his father but also by God), Solomon never forgot his mother.

---

8. Walvoord, Zuck, and the Dallas Theological Seminary, *The Bible Knowledge Commentary*. (Des Moines, WA: Biblesoft, Inc., 2015).

One might think Bathsheba's story ended at Solomon's coronation, but it did not. There was more vindication in store for her, more blessings and restoration for God to bestow on her. She became a major character in the Bible, so much so that her son wrote a book in the Bible for us that includes his mother's wisdom: Proverbs. Further, in tracing Bathsheba's life, one discovers that she became a fixture in the Kingdom of Israel (a nation that did not go to war during Solomon's reign). She sat to the right of King Solomon. That meant she had a permanent place by his side. "So, Bathsheba went to King Solomon… And the king arose to meet her, bowed before her, and sat on his throne; then he had a throne set for the king's mother, and she sat on his right" (1 Kings 2:19-20).

A woman who seemed to have lost everything was fully restored, exalted, and blessed. Still without a husband in the end, she was protected and honored all the days of her life and forever beyond, because she was included in the Lord's Word, which lasts forever (1 Peter 1:25) and "does not return empty" (Isaiah 55:11). She is mentioned in the Bible as an honorable woman, and her losses could not be compared with her achievements. God has a way of working things out for our good when we are persistent in obeying Him (Romans 8:28). We cannot always control our circumstances. We must, however, not allow them to so control us emotionally that we no longer obey God. Instead, we must demonstrate complete trust in God, no matter what we may experience. It is this mindset that refines us (James 1:2-4; 1 Peter 1:3-8) and shapes us to become powerful agents of God, because no one can control future results. Paul had horrible ministry experiences (Acts 9:16) but because of his commitment to renew his mind (Romans 12:2) and be transformed (Galatians 2:20), Paul learned to be unfazed by trouble (Philippians 4:4-7). This improved his prayer life and fostered a mindset (Philippians 4:89) that led to contentment (Philippians

4:10-12) and victorious living (Philippians 2:21; 4:13). This is why the Hebrew writer says, "run the race that is set before us'" (Hebrews 12:1-3). Paul would persistently "press towards the mark" (Philippians 3:12-21), even if it meant he had to disregard former successes as worthless (Philippians 3:7-8).

Bathsheba's life moved from pain to promise—mostly because she did not allow her past to define her. Instead, Bathsheba allowed her pain to refine her as God shaped and blessed her. Thanks be to God who turns pain into promise! The woman who became David's wife under the worst of circumstances became the mother of King Solomon who extended David's line all the way to Christ. No one of that day could have imagined such a result. When our pain does not define us, our hope and trust in God (amid trouble) refine us, and we experience the blessings of God because we decisively choose to place our full trust in Him.

Bathsheba had courage—a God-ordained commitment to do what God called her to do simply because God said she should do so. God said, "Honor the king," so Bathsheba honored the king. God said, "Listen to His prophets," so she listened to His prophets. God said, "Fight for your child," so she fought for her child. In the worst of situations, this woman did not stop functioning in a godly manner. Bathsheba was great because she respected the greatness of God, no matter what. We would all like to control the results in life, but all we can control is whether or not we surrender our lives to the King of Kings. We do not control results.

We are, most times, very aware of where we are, but when we choose to trust God and endure the race that is set before us, we can rest assured that "all things work together for the good of those who love Him" (Hebrews 12:1-4; Romans 8:28). Please note the phrase "who love Him." To love God is to keep His commandments, no matter the

34

ensuing pain or bewilderment, because, as John would go on to say, this is how we come to know Him and have His love perfected in us (John 14:15; 1 John 2:3-6).

The only fight we have in this life is the fight of faith. Paul puts it this way: "Fight **the** good fight of faith; take hold of the eternal life to which you were called, and you made the good confession in the presence of many witnesses" (1 Timothy 6:12; bold and underscore added for emphasis). Note that the verse reads, "the good fight of faith." One fight.

The Beautiful and Wise Abigail

A similar story about Abigail highlights a life surrendered to God and shows divine results, even though life's painful experiences are not removed. Abigail's story teaches that despite a woman having a passive or wicked husband, she can live successfully because of God's blessings.

Abigail was married to a man named Nabal. His parents must have known something about his potential nature at his birth because his name means "fool" or "folly." It can also be interpreted as "Evil One," and is the name for Satan / Devil. It was not that Nabal did something evil from the very beginning; it was that his very nature was evil. He was also very harsh (which in Hebrew means "cruel") when he spoke to people, and he was stubborn. Nabal's churlishness and ill-behaved nature fit his name. The Hebrew adjective for "churlish" comes from a root word that means "to be hard" or "to be severe." In Hebrew, the term for "ill-behaved" is more literally "bad [or evil] of deeds." Other renderings of these two adjectives include "surly and mean" (NRSV* and REB*), "harsh and ungenerous" (NAB*), and

35

"a hard man and an evildoer" (ᴺᴶᴾˢ*).⁹

In short, Nabal was devoid of compassion and uncaring about others' needs and what they might be going through. He said and did whatever he wanted.

The Bible teaches us that an evil person is one who has all the information and clearly knows the consequences of their actions but still chooses to do what they want. An example might be someone who inadvertently runs a red light versus another who knows it is red, understands the consequences of driving through it, but does it anyway.

We also learn that Nabal was very rich, or more literally, "very great."¹⁰ He was a wealthy, resourceful man. Please note that Nabal knew about the Word of God. He was living in the land of Caleb, who was one of the wise, committed men Moses sent into Canaan to spy it out, and Caleb remained focused on doing what God had ordered. So, Nabal's tribal history was powerful. He worked on land that God gave to Caleb because of the latter's faithfulness. This backdrop compounds how foolish, evil, and wicked Nabal chose to be.

Abigail, on the other hand, was considered beautiful and wise. She was a faithful wife, always looking out for her household even though she did not have any children. She looked out for all her servants and their families. Abigail, a woman of wisdom and beauty, stood in stark contrast to her husband and his selfish nature. Her name may mean "my father is rejoicing." The text also highlights her wisdom or "good understanding," as described in Proverbs 31:10. "Good understanding" is a noun (Heb. *sekel*) related to terms used to

* NRSV: New Revised Standard Version
* REB: Revised English Bible
* NAB: New American Bible
* NJPS TANAKH: The New Jewish Publication Society Version
9. Roger L. Omanson and John Ellington, *A Handbook on the First Book of Samuel* (New York, NY: United Bible Societies, 2001), 516. (Des Moines, WA: Biblesoft, Inc., 2015).
10. Omanson and Ellington, *A Handbook,* 516. (Des Moines, WA: Biblesoft, Inc., 2015).

describe David in contrast to Saul (1 Samuel 25:2-3). [11]

Theirs was definitely a "Beauty and the Beast" type of story. For in Abigail's culture, parents decided who their daughters married. The decision was not hers. In contemporary society, divorce would have been long sought by the woman at this point. However, Abigail had no Biblical grounds for divorce and according to the Mosaic Law, she could not divorce Nabal (Deuteronomy 24:1-5). Consequently, her married life was probably a trial every day.

Trials and tests either expose our commitment to trust God or expose the true nature of our hearts (Deuteronomy 8:2-3). Abigail proved she was not a beautiful woman merely on the outside but on the inside as well. In the case of some marriages, it may seem that there is no hope for improvement because of who the parties are on the inside. In Abigail's case, the Bible is clearly stating there was no hope for change in Nabal's heart.

In the Old Testament, 1 Samuel 25 begins with the death of Samuel, who had anointed David king. After Samuel's burial, David, who had amassed 600 men, traveled to the wilderness of Paran because Saul was constantly seeking to kill him. Then David heard that Nabal was shearing sheep in the wilderness nearby. So, David sent ten of his men to request food and provisions from Nabal since David and his men had provided protection for Nabal's shepherds. Historians have noted as follows:

> Contracts between herdsmen and sheep owners during the early part of the second millennium have been found in Mesopotamia at the town of Larsa. Herdsmen would typically receive a fee or commission on the sheep and goats that were delivered safely at the shearing.

11. Earl D. Radmacher, Ronald Barclay Allen, and Wayne H. House, *Nelson's New Illustrated Bible Commentary.* (Nashville, TN: T. Nelson Publishers, 1999). (Des Moines, WA: Biblesoft, Inc., 2015).

David's men are claiming a portion of that compensation. It would usually include wool, dairy products or grain. Nabal spurned this request and insulted David instead (1 Samuel 25:2-44).[12]

It was at that point that Nabal acted in accordance with his name: "Who is David?" he asked. "And who is the son of Jesse? There are many servants today who are breaking away from his master. Shall I then take my bread and my water and my meat that I have slaughtered for my shearers, and give it to men whose origin I do not know?" (1 Samuel 25:10-11).

When David's servant returned and relayed Nabal's message, David told his warriors, "Each of you strap on his sword.... It is certainly for nothing that I have guarded everything that this man has in the wilderness, so that nothing has gone missing of all that belonged to him! For he has returned me evil for good. May God do so to the enemies of David, and more so, if by morning I leave alive as much as one male of any who belong to him" (1 Samuel 25:13, 21-22).

However, Abigail intervened and quickly amassed enough food to feed an army—literally! She had her servants carry the provisions to David. Then Abigail showed up, prostrating on the ground before him. What she told David not only changed the course of David's destiny but afforded piercing insight into what Abigail thought of her own husband, Nabal: "Please do not let my lord pay attention to this worthless man, Nabal, for as his name is, so is he. Nabal is his name, and stupidity is with him; but I your slave did not see the young men of my lord whom you sent" (1 Samuel 25:25).

Abigail believed that God was able and chose to trust God. Four hundred of David's mighty men who would conquer the known world

---

12. Matthews, Chavalas, and Walton, *The IVP Bible Background Commentary: Old Testament* (Downers Grove, IL: InterVarsity Press, 2000). (Des Moines, WA: Biblesoft, Inc., 2015).

came against a woman and her servants. Still, Abigail placed herself in the line of fire. She trusted God by challenging David to do what was right in God's eyes. She could not ask that of her husband. By calling Nabal "worthless," she was saying Nabal was no good and lacked the ability to do good as well. He was always going to be a liar, always going to be stubborn, always going to be wicked from the minute he awoke in the morning. Everyday Nabal was going to be the harsh, mean person that he was. Being in a marriage like this exposed Abigail's character:

> In the same way, you wives, be submissive to your own husbands so that even if any of them are disobedient to the word, they may be won without a word by the behavior of their wives, as they observe your chaste and respectful behavior. Your adornment must not be merely external — braiding the hair, and wearing gold jewelry, or putting on dresses; but let it be the hidden person of the heart, with the imperishable quality of a gentle and quiet spirit, which is precious in the sight of God. For in this way in former times the holy women also, who hoped in God, used to adorn themselves, being submissive to their own husbands; just as Sarah obeyed Abraham, calling him lord, and you have become her children if you do what is right without being frightened by any fear (1 Peter 3:1-6).

Abigail then reminded David of his destiny to become king, which caused him to change course:

> "Now then, my lord, as the Lord lives, and as your soul lives, since the Lord has restrained you from shedding blood, and from avenging yourself by your own hand, now then, may your enemies and those who seek evil against my lord, be like Nabal.... And when the Lord does for my lord in accordance with all the good that He has spoken concerning you, and appoints you ruler over Israel, this will not become an obstacle to you, or a troubled heart to my lord, both by

having shed blood without cause and by my lord's having avenged himself" (1 Samuel 25:26, 30-31).

Abigail saw that her household, consisting of many servants and their families, could be destroyed. She recognized that by taking vengeful action against Nabal, David could have sinned, which would have negatively affected the dynasty with which God had blessed him. She accepted her position as a wife who had been given to a man in exchange for a dowry. She was no soldier and had no army. However, Abigail did have food, a donkey, and most importantly, the Word of God. She trusted God's Word and became a servant, a slave, placing herself in a vulnerable position where she could have been killed. In other words, Abigail preserved and kept a future king from sinning and kept her household from suffering due to an evil husband.

Bible commentator D.A. Carson noted the following about Abigail's message for David in 1 Samuel 25:26-31: "The message of Abigail's words was a theological one, making clear David's position in God's sight. We may add that her message was a very sensible one from a human standpoint as well: if David had attacked a local farmer, it is very unlikely that he would ever have won the support of the tribe of Judah at a later date."[13]

After David spared Nabal's entire household, Abigail relayed everything to Nabal once he sobered up...and Nabal had a heart attack. Ten days later, "the Lord struck Nabal and he died" (1 Samuel 25:37-38). David heard about the death and instantly proposed marriage to Abigail. She accepted, and just like that, she became David's bride, and thus a queen.

Abigail's commitment to God caused her to wait on and obey God

---

13. D. A. Carson, *New Bible Commentary: 21st Century Edition* (Leicester, England: Inter-Varsity Press, 1994). (Des Moines, WA: Biblesoft, Inc., 2015).

even when she was trapped in a bad marriage. God fought her battle in His time, and her husband eventually died. The end result was a new husband who made her a queen. Abigail was elevated from a horrible husband to a better husband, and her wealth undoubtedly increased. With David she even had children—unlike with Nabal (2 Samuel 3:3).

It should be noted that Abigail did not allow common sense or her emotions to dictate her obedience to God. She did not do what seemed convenient. She did not take the easy way out; she chose God's way. Victory is not what we create in a particular moment. It is what God provides, even if it involves waiting on Him (Isaiah 40:27-31; Romans 12:14-20).

What we learn about Abigail's inner beauty in 1 Samuel 25:2-3 is that she had strength. Not the "I'm-determined-to-make-it-through-the-day" type of strength. Hers was the type of strength that is demonstrated when, no matter the trial, one remains committed to obeying God's Word. Then again, from a human standpoint, putting her life on the line made no sense because Abigail could have used the crisis as an opportunity to get rid of Nabal. *("Free at last, free at last! Thank God Almighty she could have been free at last!")*

But it was not just about Nabal. It was about everyone else in her household. When trusting God places us in a lion's den, we are in a safe place, a powerful place, and a place of change. Trusting God involves getting out front in the firm knowledge that everything depends on His ability, not ours.

We see this same strength exhibited in Daniel. It did not matter what Daniel was experiencing, he had "made up his mind that he would not defile himself with the king's choice food or with the wine which he drank; so, he sought permission from the commander of the officials that he might not defile himself" (Daniel 1:8). We admire Daniel, but he actually benefited from the fact that God's Word is not ineffectual, and it is powerful and sharper than a double-edged sword (Isaiah 55:11; Hebrews 4:12). I believe that is what Paul meant when he said, "Therefore I am well content with weakness, with insults, with distresses, with persecutions, with difficulties, for Christ's sake; for when I am weak, then I am strong" (2 Corinthians 12:10). Paul did not endure intense suffering because He was strong (Romans 8:26). It was because Paul was convinced that with the Spirit of God powerfully working in Him, He could "do all things through Christ" (Philippians 4:13).

In contrast, Abigail was powerless, especially as a woman in Jewish culture (and had most likely entered the marriage through a dowry). So, she was not merely married to Nabal. She belonged to him. Yet, in her weakness, she trusted God, did what was right, and became strong, blessed, and delivered (Deuteronomy 8:1-20). We can fight based on our own common sense (which could be misinformed or miscalculated), but we will discover how weak we really are (Proverbs 3:4-5). A situation in which we are weak but relying on our own common sense may lead us to depression, uncontrollable anger, retaliation, or even divorce outside the will of God. Or we can choose to obey God and wait for Him to bring change. Strength is not evident when the marriage is going well. Strength is exhibited when things are very wrong, but our heart is committed to obeying God, no matter what. It is better to be in a lion's den if our obedience to God puts us there because that is when we experience His strength in our weakness. Abigail's focus was on how to make a bad situation work without running from it or finding her own way through it. We must all remember how powerful God is when we are embroiled in scathing trials: "Do you not know? Have you not heard? The Everlasting God, the Lord, the Creator of the ends of the earth does not become weary or tired. His understanding is inscrutable. He gives strength to the weary, and to him who lacks might He increases power" (Isaiah 40:28-29).

Here are four things about what strength means biblically, especially in extreme circumstances (the list is not exhaustive):

1) When the storm is raging, keep your eyes on Christ because to be victorious, persistent obedience (faithfulness to His Word) is required; this is the nature of true faith (Hebrews 11:1-12). Joseph remained in a jail when he had no clue how or when he would get out. Remember, the only fight we have is the fight of faith (1 Timothy 6:12). Will we keep God's Word? Or will we succumb to fear and lean on our own understanding?

2) Will we allow our emotions to get the best of us? David was probably afraid while facing a nine-foot-tall giant, but he believed he had victory because Goliath was a Philistine (had no covenant with God), was uncircumcised (ceremonially unclean), and taunted the army of God (anyone who cursed God's people would be cursed). All that David believed is defined by the scriptures. The army and Saul knew the Word but did not demonstrate faith by their works, whereas David did (James 2:14-26).

3) Will we fight for our rights or for God's standards? Abigail was locked in. A dowry had already been paid for her. Additionally, the Word of God, as written by Moses, gave her no way out via divorce. When things get difficult or dangerous in your life, is waiting on God the same as doing nothing? Abigail's waiting demonstrated a lot of action. Yet none of it usurped God's guidelines for how she had to behave in her marriage or with respect to Israel's future king, David.

4) Remember the promises of God during painful trials. We would do well to recall that angels minister to and serve us (Hebrews 1:14). We should also commit to memory the following line: "The angel of the Lord encamps around those who fear Him and rescues them. Taste and see that the Lord is good; how blessed is the man who takes refuge in Him" (Psalm 34:7-8).

Peter put it this way because he learned it the hard way:

"Humble yourselves, therefore, under the mighty hand of God, that He may exalt you at the proper time, casting all your anxiety upon Him, because He cares for you.... the same experiences of suffering are being accomplished by your brethren who are in the world. And after you have suffered for a little while, the God of all grace, who called you to His eternal glory in Christ, will Himself perfect, confirm, strengthen, and establish you. To Him be dominion forever and ever. Amen." (1 Peter 5:6-11; underscore added for emphasis)

When Peter finally learned to stay sober and humble himself, in due season, he was exalted to lead the disciples—first by being the one who preached at Pentecost (1 Peter 1:13-16).

God is providing us victory while refining us. That is a Biblical pattern because it is the same one we find when Job had lost everything. Can you imagine losing ten children, your business, and your health all at once (not due to something you did, but because Satan decided to test God)? Yet, Job never asked for anything back; his entire focus was on seeking an answer from God. Consider his response: "Then Job arose and tore his robe and shaved his head, and he fell to the ground and worshiped and said: 'Naked I came from my mother's womb, and naked I shall return there. The Lord gave and the Lord has taken away. Blessed be the name of the Lord.' Through all this Job did not sin nor did he blame God" (Job 1:20-22).

After reading Abigail's story, one might ask, does any wife who suffers similar experiences as Abigail become a queen? No. What this story does mean is that if God does not change your circumstances, He will use them to refine, mature, and empower you (1 Peter 1:3-11; James 1:2-4; 1 John 4:4; Romans 8:37-39). He does not just bless us in this life, but also in the life to come: "Blessed is a man who perseveres under trial; for once he has been approved, he will receive the crown of life which the Lord has promised to those who love Him" (James 1:12-13).

Let us end this chapter by reflecting on this powerful line: "He who overcomes, I will grant to him to sit down with Me on My throne, as I also overcame and sat down with My Father on His throne" (Rev 3:21-22).

CHAPTER 3
Deborah

A Woman of Valor

*I*n our era, women are sometimes repressed or struggle because of the male-dominated society. As a result, some women are stressed as they keep seeking respect for their abilities. They sometimes feel confined to roles that they may believe are beneath their potential. This is not represented in the scriptures, as we will see in the story of Deborah. What we find in Judges 4:4-22 is a woman who was a faithful wife and who also worked as a judge. She became so prominent in her service to the people of Israel that God spoke to her directly, establishing her as an ally at a very key time in Israel's history.

Before we get to the significant role Deborah played in Israel's history where male leadership was dominant, we need to provide a summary explanation of an issue that may implicitly affect how this story is viewed.

Some people use Deborah as an argument for women to be preachers when that is not the case nor the point of the passage. Deborah was a wife, mother, and prophetess, and later a judge (Judges 4:4-5; 5:7).[14] She understood who she was just by virtue of where she sat. She did not sit at the city gates where the male elders sat, nor did she walk through the streets explaining God's word to the people. Deborah sat

---

14. R. B. Hughes and J. C. Laney, *Tyndale Concise Bible Commentary* (Carol Stream, IL: Tyndale House Publishers, 2001), 100. (Des Moines, WA: Biblesoft, Inc., 2015).

"under the palm tree…between Ramah and Bethel in the hill country of Ephraim" (Judges 4:5). This well-traveled route would be a place for a judge or prophet to sit and hold court since it was also used by people going to Bethel to celebrate Passover. [15] Ramah, north of Jerusalem in Benjamin, was in the area where Samuel later judged Israel (1 Samuel 7:16).[16]

Deborah understood her role as someone who proclaimed the Word of God to the people. Theologian Warren Wiersbe says this about her:

> Part of Deborah's responsibility as a judge was to sit as arbitress in the settlement of disputes. That included fighting for the poor, for justice. She did not function as a judge of judges; meaning Deborah was not a judge in the form of Judges in the Book of Judges or in the manner Barak functioned as a deliverer of the people from foreign oppressors. Though God called Deborah to be a prophetess and a judge, she saw herself as a 'mother' to her people.…The wayward Jews were her children, and she welcomed them and counseled them. 'I, Deborah arose, that I arose a mother in Israel'. (Judges 5:7) [17]

God did not denigrate Deborah because she was a wife or someone who on her own initiative decided to judge the civil matters of the people. God is the one who reached out to Deborah (who had no official position in the nation of Israel), and made her a prophetess, a leader in Israel. Deborah was actually one of five women to be called a prophetess in the Old Testament. The others are Miriam (Exodus 15:20), Huldah (2 Kings 22:14; 2 Chronicles 34:22), Isaiah's wife (Isaiah 8:3), and Noadiah, a false prophetess (Nehemiah 6:14).

---

15. Matthews, Chavalas, and Walton, *The IVP Bible Background Commentary: Old Testament* (Downers Grove, IL: InterVarsity Press, 2000). (Des Moines, WA: Biblesoft, Inc., 2015).

16. Pfeiffer, *The Wycliffe Bible Commentary,* Judges 4:4. (Des Moines, WA: Biblesoft, Inc., 2015).

17. W. W. Wiersbe, *Be Available* (London: Victor Books, 1994), 35. (Des Moines, WA: Biblesoft, Inc., 2015).

According to Isaiah 3:12, a woman ruler was not a preferable situation for the Jews: "As for My people, children are their oppressors, and women rule over them." Further,

> "The fact that God raised up a courageous woman named Deborah to be the judge in the land was not only an act of grace, but it was also an act of humiliation for the Jews. For they lived in a male-dominated society that wanted only mature male leadership. For God to give His people a female judge was to treat them like little children, which is exactly what they were when it came to spiritual things."[18]

The words for preacher and prophet are distinctly two different Hebrew or Greek words. "Prophetess," which means "one who speaks forth," is derived from two words: "pro" (before) and "phemi" (speak). The word corresponds to the Hebrew word "nabhi," a person who speaks the will of God to people under the power of the Holy Spirit, particularly as it relates to what God plans to do in the future (Luke 1:67).[19]

As in the Old Testament, the Holy Spirit empowered prophets to reveal His will; thus they spoke with divine authority. A prophet is someone who is sovereignly chosen by God to reveal to a people the will of God. This chosen believer of God functions under the total control of the Holy Spirit of God. They do not speak on their own initiative; they only say what God has instructed them to say (Jeremiah 23:16; Ezekiel 13:1-7; Ephesians 3:1-7; 2 Peter 1:20-21). This is why we can test every prophecy (1 Thessalonians 5:19-21). The Lord takes the role seriously:

---

18. Wiersbe, *Be Available*, 34–35. (Des Moines, WA: Biblesoft, Inc., 2015).

19. *Theological Wordbook of the Old Testament*, (Chicago, IL: The Moody Bible Institute, 1980), 796. (Des Moines, WA: Biblesoft, Inc., 2015).

"Is not My word like fire?" declares the Lord, "and like a hammer which shatters a rock? Therefore behold, I am against the prophets," declares the Lord, "who steal my words from each other. Behold, I am against those who have prophesied false dreams," declares the Lord, "and reported them, and led My people astray by their false-hoods and reckless boasting; yet I did not send them or command them, nor do they furnish this people the slightest benefit," declares the Lord (Jeremiah 23:29-32).

Let us also consider the following line: "Do not be hasty in word or impulsive in thought to bring up a matter in the presence of God. For God is in heaven and you are on earth; therefore let your words be few. For the dream comes through much effort, and the voice of a fool through many words" (Ecclesiastes 5:2-3).

A preacher, however, is someone who spreads the Good News of the Gospel, whereas a prophet explains what the Lord is teaching us about the future as associated with what is written in the Old and New Testaments (2 Peter 1:19-21). In other words, both preacher and prophet interpret what God says concerning the present and the future. Preaching means "to cry out loud," "to proclaim," and "to make known: by announcing the kingdom of God in terms of a person discharging an office.[20]

It is the same as the word for "herald." These were individuals who went out under the authority of a king to proclaim the king's message to his citizens. In those days, they did not have televisions, radios, fax machines, or emails. So, when a king wanted to communicate with his citizens, he sent heralds. If they said something the king did not say, the king sent an executioner to cut off the herald's head in front of all the people. This is why Paul said, "Therefore I run in such a way, as

---

20. *Vine's Expository Dictionary of Biblical Words,* (Nashville, TN: Thomas Nelson Publishers, 1985). (Des Moines, WA: Biblesoft, Inc., 2015).

not without aim; I box in such a way, as not beating the air; but I buffet my body and make it my slave, lest possibly, after I have preached to others, I myself should be disqualified" (1 Corinthians 9:26-27).

As a prophetess, Deborah was deeply committed to diligently executing what the Lord told her to do. We do not see a record of anyone asking her to judge the people. The people were without a leader and needed answers. Deborah addressed those needs and did it so well that the people continually relied on her effective execution of the law.

Deborah did not go to law school or judge others in a courthouse. She saw a need among the people and addressed it because she was well-versed in the laws that God gave to Israel through Moses. Deborah faithfully served the people by judging the issues, based on how the laws of God related to the disputes they brought before her. She did so with such integrity and veracity the people began to rely on her even more. Deborah did such a powerful job judging the civil issues that her reputation before the people and God became significant. Thus, because of her faithful, accurate ethical interpretations of the laws of God before the people of God, she was promoted to the role of prophetess. We see this occur in Judges 6:7: "Now it came about when the sons of Israel cried to the Lord on account of Midian, that the Lord sent a prophet to the sons of Israel, and he said to them, 'Thus says the Lord, the God of Israel...' "

Where there is weak leadership, especially in times of crisis, God deploys faithful people to make a difference, regardless of whether they are men or women. Indeed, one of the first things we notice about Deborah is that she was a faithful servant of God. She served with such integrity and authority that the people throughout the nation saw and believed in her ability and knowledge.

Deborah's dedication to God manifested itself even more when she immediately did what God instructed her to do by commanding Barak to be God's deliverer for His people. This is where Deborah's leadership was revealed to be critical for the people of Israel to be delivered. Because Deborah was determined to fulfill the Lord's instructions, she kept Barak in His role while being a catalyst in fulfilling God's agenda for His people. Her relentless commitment to execute God's direction for His people continuously placed her in a position of leadership.

It should be noted that Barak was indeed called by God to be a judge, but he lacked courage. However, as a judge, Barak did not arbitrate the disputes of the people. So, Deborah's role as judge was different from how Barak functioned as a judge.

When the sons of Israel cried to the Lord, the Lord raised up a judge who was called a deliverer. This person was Barak. He was someone who raised up an army to fight against Israel's oppressors. God raised up or called judges like Barak, and then designated them to be deliverers. It was God who empowered them with His power to deliver His nation from oppression and oppressors. God is always the one to pick each judge, and subsequently, the judge leads the nation. That is why Deborah was told by God to seek out Barak.

Barak was going up against a powerful brutal oppressor named Jabin. Even though Barak clearly understood what the Lord was saying, he was obviously intimidated by the 900 chariots in Jabin's army. He was well aware of Jabin's brutality because of the twenty years over which the latter had oppressed the people of Israel. Barak's weak leadership propelled Deborah to a larger role as a judge and prophetess, which she performed without hesitation. Her determination to fulfill what God instructed her to do became the catalyst that led Barak to do what God said and later resulted in the deliverance of a nation.

It is interesting that even though Deborah eventually led the people, Barak received the credit for this momentous act in Hebrews 11:32—because God called Barak to be the judge or the deliverer. There, Barak is given an honorable mention, but Deborah is revered among her people and given more respect in the Book of Judges. There is even a song that celebrates how God used her to lead His people (Judges 5).

Deborah was a powerful woman of God who conscientiously directed Barak to do what the Lord instructed him to do. She was so dedicated to fulfilling God's direction that she accepted Barak's request to go with him to war. Her love for God inspired her to lead the people in worship before God. We must understand how distinctive this is. There were high priests, Levites, elders, and many prophets serving in the land, but God spoke through Deborah, and the people, including God's judge Barak, listened to her. For instance, when she told Barak to gather 10,000 men, even Barak, God's warrior and deliverer, did not dispute whether Deborah spoke under God's orders. With Barak's primary struggle being fear, it was a good thing he listened to Deborah, for hers was a good plan:

Apparently, the strategy commanded by Deborah and carried out by Barak was to gather the combined tribal forces at Mount Tabor, a point on the fringe of their territories, from whose heights a clear view of the area could be seen. It provided protection should they be detected too soon and allowed cover for their forces. Once they had been able to lure Sisera's army toward them through the Jezreel Valley and into the plain near the Kishon River, the Israelites could make a surprise attack on them as they floundered in the mud and water of the overflowing wadi. The strategy, as portrayed in Judges 4–5, is dependent upon divine intervention (a storm) and the giving of the exact moment in which to strike from Deborah, Yahweh's representative. [21]

No matter the challenges Deborah may have been confronted with,

21.Matthews, Chavalas, and Walton, *The IVP Bible Background Commentary: Old Testament* (Downers Grove, IL: InterVarsity Press, 2000). (Des Moines, WA: Biblesoft, Inc., 2015).

she remained faithful to God's call. She led the nation into battle not because she was a judge, a prophetess, or well-equipped to fight in war. Deborah led because she was committed to a life of faith while Barak was controlled by fear. "Courage is not the absence of fear; it is the present of faith."[22]

God put it this way when speaking to Joshua following Moses's death: "Be strong and courageous, for you shall give this people possession of the land which I swore to their fathers to give them. Only be strong and very courageous; be careful to do according to all the law which Moses My servant commanded you; do not turn from it to the right or to the left, so that you may have success wherever you go" (Joshua 1:6-8).

The issue is not about a person seeing themselves as a woman based on how the culture defines them. God gave women spiritual gifts, just like He gave men the same, and He made women in the image of God—just like He made men (Genesis 1:26-27). Therefore, women must believe it is their spiritual gifts, job skills, and commitment to faithfully serve the Lord that makes great impact in favor of God's glory. It is important to keep in mind that God promoted Deborah to a larger role because of her faithfulness in being a wife and her passionate obedience— coupled with Barak's weak leadership. It cannot be emphasized enough that Deborah's passionate commitment to obey God was the necessary ingredient to faithfully serving God. Her attitude made the deliverance of Israel a reality.

Leadership does not require an official position. A leader is someone who sees a problem and then develops a strategic plan to resolve it. Such a leader, when they remain committed to the principles of God, becomes widely recognized for their accomplishments. There are

---

22. Paul Cannings, Sermon, (Houston, Texas, March 26, 2023).

many examples of such individuals in the scriptures, such as Anna—one of only two people who was able to recognize Jesus because of her service for God. Others were Dorcas, Lydia, the four (prophetess) daughters of Philip, and many more women. Paul lists several of them in Romans 16:3, 6, and 15.

Many women were also known to support Jesus Christ during his ministry on earth (Luke 8:3). It is also remarkable that several women remained with Jesus during His crucifixion and burial and were present at His resurrection (John 19:25; 20:1; Luke 23:55-56; 24:1-10). Jesus was not considered a high priest when He was on earth, nor was he counted as even a part of the Sanhedrin. Yet, as we well know, Jesus's service blessed many lives and changed the world. He understood what God had called Him to do; He sacrificed whatever was required. Because Christ willingly complied, God exalted Him, so that at the sound of His name, "… every knee will bow, of those who are in heaven and on earth and under the earth" (Philippians 2:10).

Deborah saw a need and faithfully tried to fulfill it based on the Word of God. She never tried to usurp the authority of Barak, who was a weak leader. Her steadfast service elevated her to the position of prophetess, and later as a moral support to the military when she agreed to accompany the 10,000 men of war. As a result, she released a nation from oppression and led the process of God empowering a nation He loved once again; ultimately, she enabled Israel to experience peace for forty years thereafter (Judges 5:31). Concerning leadership, we would be wise to recall the words of our Savior:

> And hearing this, the ten began to feel indignant with James and John. And calling them to Himself, Jesus said to them, "You know that those who are recognized as rulers of the Gentiles lord it over them; and their great men exercise authority over them. But it is not

so among you, but whoever wishes to become great among you shall be your servant; and whoever wishes to be first among you shall be slave of all. For even the Son of Man did not come to be served, but to serve, and to give His life a ransom for many" (Mark 10:41-45).

Deborah is a great model because she first served when she saw a need, knew the law, and committed herself to faithfully helping her people. Her faithfulness, integrity, and effective execution of the law created respect among the people, causing them to trust her more and further establishing her as a force in Israel. She became so dominant that even the Lord God moved to elevate her to the formal role of a prophetess. When there was a weak leader, she did not try to take over from him. She kept it objective by holding Barak accountable to the Word of God. Her prior reputation and the authority of God's Word caused Barak to submit to the Word of God and move his warriors forward, even when fear had gotten the best of him. In stark contrast to his lack of courage stands Deborah's courage, which caused Barak to lean on her leadership while he fought the battle.

In some cases, women seek to acquire a position of leadership. Deborah models for us the fact that acquiring a position to lead before seeing the need to lead can be fallacious. It is how a person faithfully exercises their gifts and talents, functioning with integrity within the structure established by the Lord, that defines them as a leader. This allows their faithful service to attest to their character and spiritual maturity, leading to possible promotions as the Lord so blesses (we see this in the case of Timothy in Acts 16:1-5). This is similar to what took place with David. He refused to challenge Saul but functioned with such courage that he attained truly great accomplishments. Consequently, his reputation and achievements made it easy for the people to see God's work in his life; as a result, they chose David to become the leader of Israel. It was such an obvious choice that it was indisputable. Genuine leadership is established when those called to it respond out of respect for what they see as God's will for their life.

Deborah led the people of Israel because they recognized that she was totally surrendered to God's influence in her life. Even though Barak had the position of leadership and had been chosen by God, *she* was the key leader because of *his* lack of courage.

Leadership is not achieved because of a position we may acquire; it is displayed when we simply serve in the capacity in which we are needed—especially when it matches our spiritual gift.

CHAPTER 4
Phoebe

The Difference We Make Begins with Us

Anyone can say that they love and are committed to their family, but service is what makes family members feel loved and valued. What causes marriages and families to struggle is the absence of service.

Service triggers diverse responsibilities that make a family functional. The level of education or acclaim the family members have achieved does not matter. Someone still must clean the house, wash the dishes, and mow the lawn. In cases where families do not complete these chores personally, they hire people to do them—and the best people are those who have the attitude of a servant.

That same mindset is what makes the church a viable organism, a place where broken people can be healed and strengthened, and where the community and people around the world can be blessed (Romans 12:4-21; 1 Corinthians 12:4-31; Matthew 28:18-20). Until that happens, we are not executing God's Kingdom plan for His church, as explained in scripture.

The church, as the body of Christ, is an organism that God works through to impact the world. As stated in Ephesians 1:22-23, "And He put all things in subjection under His feet and gave Him as head over all things to the church, which is His body, the fullness of Him who fills all in all." We benefit because those who were the anchor runners in this relay were deeply committed to the Lord's agenda for His church, just as Christ was committed to God when He said, "I MUST be about MY Father's business" (Luke 2:49; capitalized for emphasis).

One of those anchor runners who ran her race in service of spreading the Lord's plan was Phoebe. She was not just the deliverer of Paul's letter to the Romans. She was known and respected as a powerful servant of God and someone trusted by the apostle Paul who said, "For me to live is Christ..." (Philippians 1:21). Paul opens Romans 16 by commending her to the believers at the church in Rome: "I recommend [commend] to you our sister Phoebe, who is a servant of the church, which is at Cenchrea, that you receive her in the Lord in a manner worthy of the saints, and that you help her in whatever matter she may have need of you; for she herself has also been a helper of many, and of myself as well" (1-2).

Paul highly valued Phoebe, a Gentile, who had neither title nor any major position in the church. From her name, we can assume that Phoebe had a pagan background since her name means "bright" or "radiant" and refers to Phoebus Apollo, the Greek god of the sun.[23] She attended a church in Cenchrea, a seaport six miles east of Corinth, whose local population was probably a mixture of Jews and Gentiles (Romans 16:1).

Though Paul never visited the church in Rome before he wrote his letter, he had apparently received much of his information about the church from Priscilla and Aquila (Acts 18:1-4).

According to early church history, the church in Rome was diverse and divided. Jews were trying to overrun the Gentiles by preaching all kinds of doctrines that were not true. For example, the author C.E.B.

---

23. Keener, *The IVP Bible Background Commentary.* (Des Moines, WA: Biblesoft, Inc., 2015).

Cranfield explains that some Jewish Christians believed their relationship with God differed from that of Gentile Christians, since they were descendants of Abraham, were circumcised, and still observed the law. To add to the confusion, Gentiles who had first converted to Judaism and later converted to Christianity were still too friendly with pagan religions. "These beliefs held by the Jewish Christians, coupled with the ignorance of the pagan and young Gentile Christians, were indicative of the nature of the church in Rome," says Cranfield.[24]

So, Paul wrote the letter to the church in Rome in response and most likely distributed it by way of Phoebe who, once she got saved, would do anything for God.

To determine exactly what Paul meant in commending Phoebe to the church at Rome, it helps to examine the Greek word he used. In the Greek text, "commends" indicates that Phoebe was recognized as a person to whom the people should pay special attention and take seriously. In our vernacular, it is an ultra-positive reference for someone. Because of the mood in the text, "commend" also denotes that Paul would continuously speak positively of Phoebe because she was a servant who had helped many.

The tense of the verb in the phrase "who is a servant" indicates Phoebe served continuously and habitually. She was a hard laborer, faithful in service to others, and functioned like someone who was dedicated to her responsibilities. Paul wanted the Roman believers to respect Phoebe because her faithful service suggested that she was consecrated, devoted, and functioning without defilement before God. She was a woman of superior moral qualities, possessing divine qualities from God as a saint.

---

24. C. E. B. Cranfield, *A Critical and Exegetical Commentary on the Epistle to the Romans* (New York: T&T Clark International, 2004). (Des Moines, WA: Biblesoft, Inc., 2015).

Phoebe, the Faithful Servant Leader

Phoebe so impressed Paul that he called her his sister and heaped more praise on her than any other woman listed in the Romans 16:3-16 passage, including Priscilla who, along with her husband Aquilla, risked her life for Paul's ministry. Indeed, so strong was Phoebe's and Paul's commitment to Christ and His agenda that it forged a bond between them. The heart of a servant, whether woman or man, is truly that of a person who has an intimate relationship with God. Without hesitation, they embody and seek to live out the following commands: "You shall love the Lord your God with all your heart, and with all your soul, and with all your mind. This is the great and foremost commandment. The second is like it, 'You shall love your neighbor as yourself'" (Matthew 22:37-39).

Phoebe did not know the people in Rome. She probably came to know Christ through Paul's ministry. She became a true disciple and, through her spiritual growth and dedicated service, a powerful leader in her community and church of Rome (John 13:34-35). That is very similar to Paul who did not know the people he wrote to in Colossians 1:3-8. Yet, he was committed to function in the manner described in Colossians 3:17: "And whatever you do in word or deed, do all in the name of the Lord Jesus, giving thanks through Him to God the Father."

The letter we call the Book of Romans is what Phoebe delivered on behalf of Paul, because many obstacles were inhibiting him from personally journeying to Rome. We look at this letter as a hallmark for helping us understand the concepts of salvation, justification, sanctification, and reconciliation, to name a few. We are blessed and excited to learn so many complex theological principles. The letter blessed the church of Rome, which had undergone many struggles and did not have the completed Canon as we do today.

It was faithful Phoebe who put her life at risk, possibly traveling past robbers on treacherous roads and overcoming many obstacles to carry Paul's letter. As a true servant of the Lord, Phoebe made it to Rome and delivered the letter into the right hands. A person whom Paul described as a true servant of the Lord seemed determined to deliver the letter so that it would bless the Roman church. One wonders if Phoebe ever imagined that what she carried would later become the Book of Romans, a book that continues to bless the Kingdom of God—now and forever. It contains the best description in the scriptures of the meaning of salvation—at least in my estimation. The agenda of the Lord for His people was extended to Rome because of this faithful woman, Phoebe.

It occurs to me that when women see male elders, male deacons, and male preachers, they might think they need to take a back seat. They may mistakenly believe they cannot become change-makers until they have a front seat, so to speak. There is no Biblical support for such a stance. It is important to keep in mind that it was the passion many women had for Christ that made a difference in progressing the spreading of the Gospel. It was women who supported Jesus's ministry that helped keep it funded (Luke 8:1-3). Thus, their passion and faithful service empowered the New Testament church, to such an extent that the church spread throughout the world.

An individual gains the title of "servant" by using their spiritual gift(s) and by displaying faithfulness to the agenda of the Lord, in and through His body and for His glory. As a result, a servant's commitment to Christ prevails regardless of their status or position in life. Phoebe remained faithful regardless of the circumstances she encountered, vividly demonstrating that she was a true servant. Paul trusted her so much and her reputation in the church at Cenchrea was so powerful that Paul had no reservations about Phoebe delivering the letter to the church in Rome. It seems he trusted her enthusiastically. In this way, one faithful woman, not seeking a title or acclaim but simply committed to the service of the Kingdom of God, did what was needed for the church when she arrived in Rome.

We may think that a servant is someone who comes and cleans our house. That is a person with a job, someone providing a service. A servant as defined in the scriptures is different and is perfectly illustrated in the actions of Jesus Christ. Imagine the King of Kings willing to hang on a cross (Mark 15:24). A true servant considers no call to be self-effacing. Jesus also modeled servanthood when He washed His disciple's dirty feet (John 13:12). He did such things to accomplish the purposes of God. As the King of Kings and Lord of Lords who knows everything, there was no job He would not do to further His Father's business (Luke 2:49). In short, personal sacrifices aside, there was nothing Christ would not do for His Father.

The Apostle Paul exhibited the same level of servanthood for the purposes of God's plan. Shipwrecked, beaten, stoned, and jailed—he persisted in spreading the Gospel to the Gentiles. Today, Gentiles are blessed because no matter the obstacles, Paul got the job done, and by the end of the Book of Acts, we are in Rome! Paul had successfully taken the Gospel (and the church) to the uttermost parts of the world (Acts 1:8).

That is the mindset that, according to Paul, Phoebe demonstrated when he described her as a servant. She was dedicated to the task, no matter the risk, because of her commitment to Christ, which caused her to deny herself and pick up her cross. That is the fundamental nature of a servant's heart; it is the natural manifestation of a true disciple (Luke 14:25-35). A servant's heart insists that the boss, Jesus Christ, is so respected and so vital that whatever He says and whatever time He requires, His agenda supersedes all else. That is why Phoebe did not need a position or a title—just the opportunity Paul provided to display the nature of her heart.

A servant is also keenly aware of the day of accountability. We are not just going to arrive in heaven, get wings, and fly around. On the day of accountability, we will stand face to face with our Master and give account of ourselves for everything He told us to do as faithful servants. When we do well, the Lord will say to us, "Well done, good and faithful servant; thou hast been faithful over a few things, I will make thee ruler over many things..." (Matthew 25:23). On the day of accountability, what will the Lord say to those who believe? This is perfectly illustrated for us in Matthew 25. What is powerful is the response of those who served: "Then the righteous will answer Him, 'Lord, when did we see You hungry, and feed You, or thirsty, and give You something to drink?" (Matthew 25:37). They did not serve for a reward; they served for the love of the Master. "Let a man regard us in this manner, as servants of Christ, and stewards of the mysteries of God. In this case, moreover, it is required of stewards that one be found trustworthy" (1 Corinthians 4:1-3).

A person who has a genuine relationship with God will naturally serve Him out of love and reverence for Him. The more we fall in love with God, the more we worship and serve Him because we continuously die to ourselves: "So then, none of you can be My disciple who does not give up all his own possessions. Therefore, salt is good; but if even salt has become tasteless, with what will it be seasoned? It is useless either for the soil or for the manure pile; it is thrown out. He who has ears to hear, let him hear" (Luke 14:33-35).

Our spiritual gift defines our service, and the Lord has provided a spiritual gift to all believers based on His own measure (1 Peter 4:7-11; Ephesians 4:7; 2 Corinthians 10:13). Moreover, He has provided the Holy Spirit so that we have "all spiritual blessings" (Ephesians 1:3-4). So, there is no need for us to compare ourselves with others—to do so is sin (2 Corinthians 10:12-13; James 4:17). We just need to run our races well, based on what He has called us to do, because we are expected to be His servants (Colossians 3:17). As we live each day, are we going to spend that time fighting for titles and positions? Or are we going to remember what the Lord says and work while it is day, knowing there is a time to live and a time to die (John 9:4-5; Ephesians 5:15-17)?

The Lord bestows eternal blessings upon the person with a true servant's heart. Some of those rewards include receiving an everlasting crown, sharing His throne, and more (2 Timothy 4:6-8; Revelation 3:21-22). However, there is no reward for doing things our way...and there is no purgatory to fix it (1 Corinthians 3:10-15).

After such an extensive discussion about servanthood, one might ask, "What type of service did Phoebe render to the early church?" It is believed Phoebe was a deaconess in the church in Cenchrea, her duties including meeting the spiritual and material needs of believers.[25] Bible commentator C.E. Arnold says as follows:

Probably Paul identifies Phoebe as one of the deacons in the Cenchrean church. In later centuries, the office of "deaconess" was officially recognized. But the masculine *diakonos* was also applied to female officeholders in the early church. The New Testament reveals little about the role of deacons in the church, but many scholars suspect that they are particularly involved in visiting the sick, providing for the needy, and caring for the financial and material needs of the church in general. Such a function would suit well Phoebe's apparent secular position.[26]

---

25. Charles F. Pfeiffer and Everett Falconer Harrison, *The Wycliffe Bible Commentary: New Testament* (Chicago: Moody Press, 1962). (Des Moines, WA: Biblesoft, Inc., 2015).

26. C. E. Arnold, *Zondervan Illustrated Bible Backgrounds Commentary: Romans to Philemon* (Vol. 3) (Grand Rapids, MI: Zondervan, 2002), 91. (Des Moines, WA: Biblesoft, Inc., 2015).

Phoebe, the Patron and Helper

It is believed that Phoebe's secular career was related in scope to the type of service she rendered to the church. For the word Paul uses to describe her denotes "helper" or "succorer," besides also suggesting that she was perhaps a legal representative, a lawyer. The Latin equivalent *"patronus"* means someone who is a legal representative of a foreigner. Thus, one commentator says, "Phoebe was a person of some wealth and position who was thus able to act as patroness of a small and struggling community."[27]

Upon her arrival, Paul instructed the believers in Rome to not only welcome Phoebe but also to "…help her in whatever matter she may have need of you; for she herself has also been a helper of many, and of myself as well" (Romans 16:2). Bible commentator James Denney remarks as follows: "Paul's language suggests that Phoebe was going to Rome on business in which the Roman saints could assist her. 'Succourer' is *'prostatis*, 'a woman set over others, a protectress, a patroness,' caring for the affairs of others and aiding them with her resources."[28]

Phoebe could have been an advocate for the poor, the indigent, the hurting, and those who were being abused by wealthy aristocrats via heavy taxation in the country. In fact, that could have been one of the main reasons Paul highly recommended Phoebe to a prominent church in Rome. Paul asked this faithful woman who was going to Rome (possibly to litigate for a client) to carry his letter to the Roman church, while simultaneously letting the believers in Rome know Phoebe was one of the Lord's faithful servants.

---

27. W. Sanday, and Arthur C. Headlam, *A Critical and Exegetical Commentary on the Epistle of the Romans*, 3d ed., (New York, NY: C. Scribner's sons, 1897). (Des Moines, WA: Biblesoft, Inc., 2015).

28. Kenneth S. Wuest, *Wuest's Word Studies from the Greek New Testament: For the English Reader*. (Grand Rapids, MI: Eerdmans, 1984). (Des Moines, WA: Biblesoft, Inc., 2015).

In Romans 16:2, Paul wrote, "...that you receive her in the Lord." He was writing to Gentiles and Jews, knowing the Jews might not see Phoebe as a viable representative of God because of her pagan background. (Romans chapters 9 through 11 discusses the trouble between Jews and Gentles during that time.) Thus, with the authority of an apostle, Paul instructed them to accept Phoebe as a faithful believer because she was tested and proven true.

Phoebe became a difference maker, which is why Paul said Phoebe should be received, "...in a manner worthy of the saints" (Romans 16:2). Now let us assess how the word "worthy" can be related to the process of weighing something on a scale. For example, if a person needs a pound of sugar, a one-pound weight is put on one side of the scale to make sure it accurately measures a pound of sugar. So what is Paul saying? He is saying, in effect, "When I look at the Hall-of-Fame saints in heaven, Phoebe is pound for pound equal with them." In Paul's estimation, Phoebe stands alongside all the believers going to heaven, where there is no distinction between male and female (Acts 2:17-18).

Some believers assign a higher pedigree to themselves because of their gender, biblical knowledge, or degrees attained. However, that thought does not hold up against the scriptures. Knowledge, left to itself, only makes believers arrogant and useless to God, according to 1 Corinthians 8:1-2 and 1 Peter 5:5-6. As a woman, Phoebe is included in the cloud of witnesses, highly esteemed in the eyes of God. She may not have had the credentials many people today associate with greatness, but her faith in Christ and her service for the Lord, helped her ascend to a whole new level of respect.

Saints are people with servants' hearts, as displayed in their commitment to live under the authority of the scripture, especially during intense trials. They effectively use their spiritual gifts in God's arena—the church—with the aim of blessing others and progressing the Kingdom of God to ultimately transform the world. They live holy, separated unto God (1 Corinthians 1:2). Saints are willing to be changed by God each day, through the transforming work of the Holy Spirit (Romans 8:9-17; 1 Peter 1:13-16). They have a reverence for God that enables them to live out the principles of God, no matter the sacrifice required, so that by dying to themselves they become more and more like Christ. This should actually be every believer's goal (Colossians 1:28-29; 1 Peter 2:9).

> And Jesus answered them, saying, 'The hour has come for the Son of Man to be glorified. Truly, truly, I say to you, unless a grain of wheat falls into the earth and dies, it remains by itself alone; but if it dies, it bears much fruit. He who loves his life loses it; and he who hates his life in this world shall keep it to life eternal. If anyone serves Me, let him follow Me; and where I am, there shall My servant also be; if anyone serves Me, the Father will honor him' (John 12:23-26).

That is who Phoebe was in the eyes of the Lord, forever separated from others to God and blessed forever. In effect, Paul was expressing that because of Phoebe's character and faithful service, she had become someone of great value to the church: a saint.

We are at a point in our history where believers are more committed to political parties than to Christ and His church. People knock on doors to push a party's agenda but are too afraid to knock on doors to extend God's plan. Further, many believers give more money to political parties than to the church or para-church ministries. Believers today behave like Israelites who pushed to have a king (Saul), as if the Lord God was not good enough. Israel wanted to be like other nations rather than simply being God's nation—which meant they would always be different, a fact they could not accept.

In contrast, the saints who are set aside for God's agenda are, like

Christ, totally committed to making whatever sacrifices are required to accomplish His purposes. They view God's way as the only way and the church as His answer for everything (Ephesians 1:22-23). Not counting all the contributions she made on behalf of the people in her community (besides probably holding down a job), Phoebe became a valued member of the church because her life was totally dedicated to completing whatever God directed her to do.

In these last days, as we move closer to the return of Christ, there is so much pain and false doctrine, and so many broken relationships, angry children, and dysfunctional families. What God needs are more Phoebes, not women who need a title to serve Him. Rather, He needs saints, passionate about spreading the gospel, strengthening broken souls, guiding bewildered believers, and transforming congregations, thereby rising to become significant parts of propagating God's Kingdom. Stop and take a moment to read Matthew 25:31-46. Now, where in that passage does it say that serving Christ only applies to men?

After the eleven disciples forsook Christ (after three years of seminary training by the Master Himself), we find four ladies at the cross. It did not matter that the earth shook, that dead saints came back to life, and that darkness pervaded the skies. Their love for Christ and dedication to the Lord's cause revealed their bravery, dedication, and submission to the will of God. Women are an important work force for God's Kingdom agenda.

So, never look at yourself and ask, *What can I do as a woman?* Discover your spiritual gift based on how the Lord has equipped you to serve Him faithfully. Spiritual maturity opens our eyes to see (1 Corinthians 2:10-15). The growing use of our spiritual gifts makes us useful to the Lord. Christ gave His disciples obstacles to overcome and tasks to accomplish. His group of leaders declined from seventy men to eleven and eventually to twelve. It was not until they were completely committed to being His disciples that He placed them in positions of leadership (Matthew 19:27-30).

It is not that women should not hold positions in the church because Pheobe did. That is NOT what I am saying. What is mostly displayed by Pheobe, Deborah, or Bathsheba is the nature of a leader that God promotes. When these attitudes are viably present and demonstrated, the kingdom agenda of God is not impeded by any means, and obstacles do not encumber progress. Leaders were in place when Christ was on earth but instead of them welcoming Christ (they knew who He was as per John 5:39), they brutally nailed Him to a cross, thereby displaying no spiritual insight, selfish leadership traits, jealousy, and hunger for power.

It was the sailors, tax collectors, abusers and murderers of the church (like Paul), and women who were heroes progressing the work of the kingdom of God who made the difference. This is why Paul, who wrote half the New Testament, would express more about how he became more like Christ as he pressed towards the mark—rather than how great of an apostle he was. "Therefore, my beloved brethren, be steadfast, immovable, always abounding in the work of the Lord, knowing that your toil is not in vain in the Lord" (1 Corinthians 15:58).

The difference women can make is exposed by the impact the Lord has established in their hearts and the love nurtured by His powerful movement in their lives (John 13:34-35).

CHAPTER 5
Lydia

Purposeful

A few years ago, my wife and I traveled to China where we visited several historical buildings. As we were standing in China Square, I asked the guide, "How in the world did they get some of these things in here years ago?" The guide said that it sometimes took builders years to transfer the materials via horses. He also said that centuries ago, building materials were made in one piece, and it could take years to install them because some of the buildings were made without nails.

A similar story emerges about a traveler seen standing in front of a great cathedral in Rome. Ogling the details in the ceiling, beams, towers, posts, and murals, the traveler asked the guide, "This must have taken years to design … What made them invest so much time, energy, mental ingenuity, and persistence to finish a project this enormous?" The guide paused and said, "Passion. Passion is what made the difference. Passion for a god or emperor they believed in, passion for what they wanted to establish for a momentous purpose."

From a different perspective, Jesus was a carpenter in a small city called Jerusalem. This Jesus Christ died on an old rugged cross, slaughtered by Roman soldiers and rejected by a people He came to save after demonstrating His supernatural power daily. Now, after 2000 years, people cannot stop talking about Him. How could this God-man come to earth, perform miracles, and work the way He did, yet change the world without social media, Internet, television, or radio? Passion. Jesus Christ had a passion that was intentional and all-consuming, because "God so loved the world..." (John 3:16).

The church today must learn to be as intentional as believers in the scriptures. It is not that we lack the trait of intentionality because we demonstrate it in our love for our jobs, educational achievements, material acquisitions, and physical health. We are simply not as purposefully driven toward the teachings of God compared to many people in the scriptures. That is why I am examining this woman named Lydia. I pray her life inspires you. Of all the people Christ could have included in the Bible, He selected Lydia to teach us how one woman can make a difference.

The apostle Paul and Timothy, his son in the faith, were ministering in Phillipi, a city in Macedonia. On the Sabbath, they visited the riverside and encountered several women:

> ...we sat down and began speaking to the women who had assembled. A woman named Lydia was listening; she was a seller of purple fabrics from the city of Thyatira, and a worshiper of God. The Lord opened her heart to respond to the things spoken by Paul. Now when she and her household had been baptized, she urged us, saying, 'If you have judged me to be faithful to the Lord, come into my house and stay.' And she prevailed upon us (Acts 16:13-15).

The ancient historian Josephus says that far more women than men in that region were attracted to Judaism. Furthermore, Bible commentator Craig Keener explains that women living in Macedonia exercised more freedom than their Greek counterparts. Keener goes on to say, "But Greek religion consisted of ritual, not teaching; thus, these women would have had little training in the law and would welcome

Paul's teaching—although his teaching a group of women might violate traditional Palestinian protocol."[29]

As a businesswoman, Lydia traversed among the Jews regularly, especially the financially affluent ones. Through her interactions with the Jews, Lydia witnessed their commitment to God and how it affected the way they lived. Thus, she became a dedicated worshipper of God in an Old Testament context. Her involvement in worship among the Jews was habitual, meaning she was very faithful and committed to worshipping with them. Though she did not fully convert to Judaism, she wanted to learn more about the God the Jews loved. This prepared her heart, such that when she heard Paul, she was fully committed. Ultimately, Lydia became the first European recorded in scripture to have accepted Jesus Christ as her Savior and Lord.

So intentional was Lydia concerning her faith that she found a way to impact her own family. Her entire family lived in a way that pleased God; therefore she could ask the apostle Paul, whom she saw as a man of God, to come into her home and meet her family. It was as if she was saying, "Look at what you see in my family. Look at me. In closer quarters—not on the street, not inside of the Jewish temple or synagogue, not in any of those places. But you come within my personal life, and you tell me what you find." That is the person who makes the difference, the one who is the same outside their home as inside it.

The word "urged" in the text suggests that she wanted Paul to stop spending money on accommodations and use her house as his base of operations for ministry in Thyatira. She literally looked at Paul and Timothy and said, "Get in my house. I have a room for you to stay in and servants who can assist you." Paul, in effect, responded, *"No. We do not want to be a burden to anybody."* (Remember, Paul sold tents

29. Craig Keener, *IVP Bible Background Commentary: New Testament* (Downers Grove, IL: InterVarsity Press, 1993). (Des Moines, WA: Biblesoft, Inc., 2015).

75

to sustain his ministry.) Lydia insisted they remain at her house, and Paul and Timothy finally relented and stayed with her, stating that "she prevailed upon us" (Acts 16:15).

> Paul and his companions may have been staying at an inn till the sabbath, but Lydia immediately offers the proper Jewish hospitality and invites the apostles into her home, thus serving as a patron of their work (cf. 1 Ki 17:13-24; especially 2 Ki 4:8-11). She appears to be the head of a household consisting mainly of servants, but it is also possible that she is married to a husband who simply leaves her religious activities alone (contrast the usual custom in Ac 16:31-32; cf. 2 Ki 4:8-23).[30]

The scripture says this of Lydia: "The Lord opened her heart to respond to the things spoken by Paul" (Acts 16:14). The Greek text helps us understand how motivated Lydia became. The Greek word for "open up" means "...to be willing to learn and evaluate fairly, to open someone's mind, to cause someone to be open-minded."[31] Scripture teaches that after the resurrection, Jesus opened the minds of the disciples to understand the scriptures (Luke 24:45); similarly, God opened Lydia's heart to respond to the Gospel message of Paul.

We can also surmise that God opened her heart because Lydia was intentional and sincere about her walk with God. That is what created her legacy which eventually impacted the whole of Europe. God continually blessed her—to the point where Lydia built a large home where saints gathered, leading to her house becoming a church (Acts 16:40). According to Bible commentator J.B. Polhill,

---

30. Keener, (Des Moines, WA: Biblesoft, Inc., 2015).

31. *Greek-English Lexicon Based on Semantic Domain.* (New York: United Bible Societies, 1988). (Des Moines, WA: Biblesoft, Inc., 2015).

...she did not merely open her home to the missionaries; she allowed it to become the gathering place for the entire Christian community (v. 40). Perhaps the wealthiest member of the Philippian church, Lydia embraced the ideal of the early church, not laying claim to what was hers but freely sharing it with her sisters and brothers in Christ.[32]

God's blessings did not deter her; instead, His blessings empowered her to be more effective and useful for the Kingdom of God. Thus, Lydia became a difference-maker in Philippi, a leading city in the district of Macedonia, and in Thyatira, from where she secured her purple fabric (Acts 16:12, 14).

"There is no record that Lydia was married, and it is unknown if she was a widow, but the members of her household may refer to her children or her servants. What is clear is that she was a woman of means due to the size of her house, which had enough space and rooms to house four missionary men and her entire household."[33]

As a single woman, Lydia had a very profitable business selling purple fabric. The people of her day liked purple so much that they wore it repeatedly. Her business expanded, and soon she was selling the material to the Jews in Philippi. Lydia became independently wealthy in the same sense as someone of our time being called a "self-made" woman or man. Of her occupation, Keener said as follows:

Lydia is well-to-do as a seller of purple, a luxury good associated with wealth throughout Mediterranean culture for over a thousand years. (The dye had been especially procured from the murex shellfish near Tyre, but in Macedonia it could have been procured from the

32. J. B. Polhill, *Acts*, Vol. 26 (Broadman & Holman Publishers, 1992), 349–350. (Des Moines, WA: Biblesoft, Inc., 2015).

33. S. D. Toussaint, "Acts," in *The Bible Knowledge Commentary: An Exposition of the Scriptures,* eds. J. F. Walvoord and R. B. Zuck (Victor Books, 1985), 399. (Des Moines, WA: Biblesoft, Inc., 2015).

mollusks near Thessalonica.) Well-to-do women sometimes became patrons, or sponsors, of pagan religious associations; those attracted to Judaism helped support Jewish causes.[34]

Despite Lydia's entrepreneurship, which involved frequent travel, she seems to have never allowed her commercial endeavors to interfere with her time before God and in service to Him. Lydia invested not only time but also her energy and resources. It was her passion for God that led to her passion for Jesus Christ, making her service habitual, though not in the sense of a ritual habit. No, Lydia's was a passionate desire to intentionally allow the Savior she encountered and accepted to become Lord of her life.

Lydia was a very influential woman who didn't view her singleness as a weakness. To the contrary, her singleness was her strength. Many times, women view their singleness as a weakness rather than a strength. Based on 1 Corinthians 7:32-35, Paul viewed his singleness as an advantage, not a weakness. It promoted someone in God's eyes, the whole idea being to "secure undistracted devotion to the Lord" (verse 35). Thus, Lydia was not concerned that she was single. She used her status to invest in and develop a viable ministry for God. Being single is definitely not a negative thing—as modeled by various individuals in the scriptures. Many saw it as a positive advantage that freed up their time and energy for the development of God's Kingdom.

I asked my oldest sister Ruth Ann Cannings, who lives in England and who has been single all her life, if she would ever marry. Her response startled me: "That would mess me up with all that I am doing and feel called to do." For context, Ruth Ann travels all over the world preaching and teaching in various capacities within her denomination and serves in key leadership roles in her church.

---

34. Keener, *IVP Bible Background Commentary*. (Des Moines, WA: Biblesoft, Inc., 2015).

Another sister, Dr. Elisabeth Cannings, is also single and works as a personal assistant to Dr. Tony Evans. She believes that if she were married, there would be no possible way she could have done all that she has accomplished for the more-than-forty years she has served in ministry. She assisted my other sister, the late Dr. Lois Evans, with her children so Lois could travel with her husband, Dr. Tony Evans, as they performed ministry together for years. Elizabeth built her life, by the grace of God, on her own. She purchased her own home and completed a PhD before retiring from a thirty-year service in the children's ministry at Oak Cliff Bible Fellowship Church, Dallas, Texas.

My other sister Bernice Cannings, who is also single, has owned her business for years. Yet, she has faithfully served in her church the whole time.

I must also mention my administrative assistant Gail O'Neal who, upon her husband's passing, decided to remain single and is a powerful, quiet source of support for me in ministry. The hours and effort she contributes (that have had nothing to do with her job description), truly exemplify her commitment to the church.

Similarly, Lydia used her singleness to be very productive in her business and in ministry. She seems to have been very kind to those who served in her home and business. Thus, God saw her heart and blessed her to have a passion for Him, which in turn made her intentional about building not just her business but also the work of the Lord Jesus Christ.

I am not saying, by any means, that a person should not seek to be married. If the Lord provides the opportunity, use the marriage He provided as a service to Him, so it becomes a blessing to you, your husband, and (if the Lord provides) your subsequent family. What is needed is for those whom the Lord allows to be single not to spend each day hoping to be married. First, as Paul would teach, focus on cultivating undistracted devotion to the Lord (1 Corinthians 7:32-35). His single life led to multiple churches being established and half the New Testament being written. Sure enough, Peter, who was married, also accomplished a lot, but not to the extent Paul did.

The point is that today, we chase blessings rather than the Blesser. Churches blossom today on promises that God will bless us if we do this or that. Rather, we should seek to *be* a blessing, especially since He saved us from hell and saves us from Satan's daily attempts to destroy us. The Lord poured His Holy Spirit into us (Titus 3:4-8), so that we can communicate with the Lord and grow in Him daily. This is our biggest victory against a common enemy, Satan (1 John 4:4). If we had Lydia's mindset, perhaps we would make a major difference in the lives of those around us, if not throughout the world.

Lydia and the Apostle Paul

In Acts 9, Paul gets converted, and in chapter 15, the apostles and elders resolve the issue of whether Gentiles were to be included in the church. At the end of the meeting, the apostles write a letter to the Gentiles and send Paul, Barnabus, Silas, and Judas to deliver it to Antioch, the Gentile city where believers were first referred to as "Christians." One of the Gentiles who helped Paul accomplish what he did was this single woman, Lydia. On Paul's first mission trip under the authority of the elders and apostles, Lydia's passion for the Lord made the first Christian impact in Europe a reality. This single woman, who was no world leader or major political player in Thyatira, was included in the New Testament for her passion and intentional work which enabled the spread of God's Word and Kingdom agenda throughout Europe. Her passion for God, born among the Jews and solidified through her association with Paul, created a long-lasting legacy.

The town of Thyatira was not far from Philippi. The church here is the same church many people believe was mentioned in Revelation 2. Though Paul founded the church in Thyatira, Lydia was the one who inspired it by first encouraging Paul to stay at her home. Lydia's business expertise and financial resources, coupled with her large home, became the foundation upon which this church was established. Though the church thrived at the beginning, by the time of Revelation 2, it was struggling with false doctrine and immorality. Yet, it was still in existence, and many still believed and were committed to Christ:

> But I say to you, the rest who are in Thyatira, who do not hold this teaching, who have not known the deep things of Satan, as they call them—I place no other burden on you. Nevertheless, what you have, hold fast until I come. And he who overcomes, and he who keeps My deeds until the end, to him I will give authority over the nations; and he shall rule them with a rod of iron, as the vessels of the potter are broken to pieces, as I also have received authority from My Father; and I will give him the morning star. He who has an ear, let him hear what the Spirit says to the churches (Revelation 2:24-29).

Lydia was not in a church-led environment (as the Jews were in Philippi). She was caught in a pagan-polluted system where people were worshipping in many pagan temples. She lived in a small city run by the Romans, a city replete with immorality, where all pleasures were available to whoever wanted to enjoy them. That is why Paul had to deal with the demon-possessed slave girl, which led to Paul's imprisonment and presentation before the court for "...proclaiming customs which it is not lawful for us to accept or to observe being Romans" (Acts 16:21). Upon getting out of jail miraculously, and despite the fact that his jailer got saved, Paul was asked to leave the city as soon as he was released. That is why by the time of Revelation, the church had become polluted by the surrounding culture.

Interestingly, what was prevalent during Jezebel's time spanning from 1 Kings 16 to 2 Kings 9 was what we see in the church of Thyatira in Revelation 2. Pagan religious beliefs penetrated Thyatira as aggressively as in the Old Testament when Jezebel introduced the Baal religion.

Lydia, who was not an elder, deacon or pastor, wielded such an influence in the church that upon their release from jail, Paul and Silas first went to Lydia's house, joining "the brothers and sisters" gathered there (Acts 16:40). This is very similar to what happened when Peter was released from prison and went to the home of John Mark's mother Mary in Acts 12:11-17. Here's another woman who used her home to serve the Lord. Her influence motivated her son to become a faithful servant of the Lord God (Colossians 4:10; 2 Timothy 4:11).

Lydia used her entrepreneurship, financial resources, employees, and the house she lived in to help establish a growing ministry in the midst of paganism and Roman power. Again, even though she was a business owner, her involvement with and service to the church was not diminished by a lack of time or by her success. Indeed, her business acumen became a stabilizing force that held the church together. Moreover, Lydia perfectly fulfilled the exhortation to wealthy saints in 1 Timothy 6:17-19:

> Instruct those who are rich in this present world not to be conceited or to fix their hope on the uncertainty of riches, but on God, who richly supplies us with all things to enjoy. Instruct them to do good, to be rich in good works, to be generous and ready to share, storing up for themselves the treasure of a good foundation for the future, so that they may take hold of that which is life indeed.

That helps us to come to grips with the kind of environment in which Lydia intentionally and passionately developed the church. It could have cost her dearly—especially in terms of her business—but Lydia's passion for Christ eclipsed those concerns. Similarly, once Paul's passion for Christ dominated his life, Paul counted earthly accomplishments as nothing (Philippians 3:3-11).

Sometimes we bring ourselves before God, but still cannot see who He is. As rich and influential as she was, Lydia risked business because of her decision to follow Christ in that culture. Still, her passion to serve Christ was above everything. She saw Christ for who He is and, as a result, was willing to listen. Lydia had a heart for God, and it became a powerful experience for her and all those who were served by her ministry. Notice that "…the Lord opened her heart," not her mind (Acts 16:14). The Lord had already opened her mind, but her heart was not yet opened, meaning she still practiced the rituals of Judaism but did not experience a major lifestyle change until she accepted Jesus Christ as her Savior.

"Women like Lydia were particularly prominent in Paul's missionary efforts in this portion of Acts—the women of Thessalonica (Acts 17:4) and of Berea (Acts 17:12), Damaris in Athens (Acts 17:34), and Priscilla in Corinth (Acts 18:2). Priscilla and Lydia took an active role in the ministry of their churches. This was in part due to the more elevated status of women in the contemporary Greek and Roman societies. This was particularly true in the first century when women were given several legal privileges, such as power to initiate divorce, sign legal documents, and even hold honorary public titles. Women's prominent role in Acts was perhaps strengthened by the message Paul brought them: "In Christ Jesus, there is neither male nor female" (Galatians 3:28)."[35]

Many hear the Word but ignore it—just like the High Priest and other Jewish leaders who nailed Christ to the cross even though they

---

35. Polhill, *Acts,* 349. (Des Moines, WA: Biblesoft, Inc., 2015).

knew who He was (John 5:39-40). Knowledge, left to itself, festers and births arrogance (1 Corinthians 8:1-2). It takes a heart surrendered to Christ to bring about a Spirit-led lifestyle change (Ephesians 3:16-21; 5:15-18). That was proven when Jesus walked on earth. How could a man do good every day, healing people, teaching them the scriptures, blessing people in their homes, and raising people from the dead—yet still be nailed to a cross and crucified? And the people supported all this when the Romans were oppressing them with heavy taxation, and the temple was corrupt. These tragic events happened because the minds of the people were engaged with the Bible, but their hearts were never changed. So, instead of welcoming the Messiah, they crucified Him.

It is similar to recruiting a player for a particular football team who secretly wishes he were playing for another team. He learns the playbook, attends all the practice sessions, and plays in all the games, yet the true desire is to play on another team he has aspired to since childhood. When one plays for the team of their childhood dreams, their heart is entirely absorbed…and they play with passion. Lydia was on the team of her dreams; she was all in, no matter the risks or challenges. As a result, Lydia made the ministry of the church of Thyatira a great place to grow.

Lydia's passion for God's Kingdom agenda caused her to not only discern the need for the church in Thyatira but also to understand the mission the Lord gave Paul. In Acts 16:15, Lydia asked Paul to judge her based on how she had functioned in serving them. By using the word "judged," Lydia demonstrated a level of confidence because of how she had served and lived before Paul and Timothy. She knew that she had been at her very best before them.

How many of us can say that? Here was a worshipper of God, one they called a Proselyte, who listened to the Bible, believed the Bible and was passionately committed to the Bible. Lydia was such a leader in her home as a single woman. She could invite a man who was an apostle of God into her home and say, "Judge my house and tell me what you find." If she was found trustworthy, she wanted to know how to assist Paul and Timothy in accomplishing their ministry, being determined to see it through. Lydia said to Paul and Timothy, "Come into my house and stay" (Acts 16:15). In other words, since Paul's ministry brought her to Christ, she wanted others to experience the same. So, she was an influential leader both in the home and the church, and her singleness was not a handicap.

Because Lydia's home became the base for Paul's work, his ministries in Thyatira and Philippi were productive then and even now. And she did not stop there. Many believe Lydia was the one who supported Paul when he was completely depleted of funds in Philippi. For, according to 2 Corinthians 8:1-7, the Macedonians were poor, beyond poverty, but Epaphroditus brought gifts from them to Paul:

> You yourselves also know, Philippians, that at the first preaching of the gospel, after I left Macedonia, no church shared with me in the matter of giving and receiving except you alone; for even in Thessalonica, you sent a gift more than once for my needs. Not that I seek the gift itself, but I seek the profit which increases to your account. But I have received everything in full and have an abundance; I am amply supplied, having received from Epaphroditus what you have sent, a fragrant aroma, an acceptable sacrifice, pleasing to God. And my God will supply all your needs according to His riches in glory in Christ Jesus. (Philippians 4:15-20).

Because Lydia kept engaging in ministry, even when Paul was in prison, she ensured the Lord's agenda impacted the world. Thus, Paul, who wrote half the New Testament, was empowered by a single woman named Lydia. We read Paul's writings today and through them, we are still being blessed by Lydia, the woman behind the scenes.

Lydia may not have become well known, but once saved, hers was a life well lived. Hers was a life that created such an impact for God's glory that the Lord made sure she was mentioned in scripture because of her passionate dedication to His agenda. Europe heard the Word of God because Lydia provided a home base for the great apostle, Paul.

In the many years of my service in ministry, I have seen many women live their whole lives with the sole aim of getting married— when the largest work force in any church across the globe are women. Even at Golgotha, there were more women than men who remained at the cross with Christ. In most cities, there are more women than men (does not seem like this can be accidental when every child is a gift from God, as stated in Psalm 127:3). Further, the Lord makes it clear that men are not to have more than one wife (Deuteronomy 17:17) as that would muddy the correlation of the Church being the bride of Jesus Christ. So, it is obvious that Christ, through whom all things come to be (Colossians 1:15-18), has decided that many women will be single. I cannot emphatically say that His purpose is to have more Lydias, but I can theorize that such a conclusion would definitely make sense, since historically, women have exerted tremendous impact in the service of the Lord. Many times in biblical history, they have carried the burden of ministry:

A widow is to be put on the list only if she is not less than sixty years old, having been the wife of one man, having a reputation for good works; and if she has brought up children, if she has shown hospitality to strangers, if she has washed the saints' feet, if she has assisted those in distress, and if she has devoted herself to every good work. But refuse to put younger widows on the list, for when they feel sensual desires in disregard of Christ, they want to get married, thus incurring condemnation, because they have set aside their previous pledge. At the same time, they also learn to be idle, as they go around from house to house; and not merely idle, but also gossips and busybodies, talking about things not proper to mention. Therefore, I want younger widows to get married, bear children, keep house, and give the enemy no occasion for reproach; for some have already turned aside to follow Satan. If any woman who is a believer has dependent widows, she must assist them and the church must not be burdened, so that it may assist those who are widows indeed. (1 Timothy 5:9-16).

I agree that in our context today, that passage seems belittling to women and therefore deserves an exegetical explanation. Please note that the meaning it may seem to communicate on the surface will not be accurate. So please, take time, if you need it, to find a very good commentator to guide you through its meaning. Please take the time to understand without becoming offended and turning away from it.

Yes, it is obvious from Genesis that God chose men to be in key positions of leadership. However, men would not be able to fulfill their callings without "leaders in heels." My wife, who purposefully does not want to be out front, has been a constant participant in the church we have founded, and I have pastored for thirty years (at the writing of this book). She made considerable personal sacrifices for us as a family and to get the church off the ground. She has done so while being a very good mother, an employee managing two pre-schools (a Christian school and an after-school program), and a wife helping her husband continuously (the list goes on). I would not even have the seminary and post-graduate education that I do were it not for her willing sacrifice. And it's not just my wife, my mom and Sister Clark who inspire respect as notable women of God. The list is far too long to name the others.

In college, I used to act in plays. During that time, I realized that if the people behind the scenes did not do their jobs effectively, the entire production would not be as riveting as the audience would prefer. It was the people behind the scenes who made the audience occasionally want to give us actors a standing ovation. Not all women in the Bible were behind the scenes, but many of them were. We will spend the next chapter talking about these female heroes that the Lord made sure are included in the scriptures.

CHAPTER 6
Unseen Heroes

O ne day, while I was rushing to board a plane, I noticed a lot of soldiers near the departure gate. I was so busy trying to board the plane that I forgot to do what I had promised my brother Joey I would do whenever I saw soldiers: thank these men and women for their service.

My brother, a twenty-four-year Army veteran, had informed me about the difficulties men and women of the armed forces face each day as they serve the country. These men and women give up control of their own lives. In an instant, they are deployed to war, sometimes never to see their families again. That is because the country's agenda is their first priority.

Similarly, Jesus faithfully, relentlessly, and comprehensively executed the agenda of God. That is why on Calvary's Cross, He said, "It is finished." His sacrifice will never be forgotten. However, because He was fully human and had all the needs a normal human being would have, there were some forgotten heroes who should also be remembered. This chapter sheds light on the women who accompanied Christ and supported Him during His earthly ministry.

Consider the primary passage that references them: "...the twelve were with Him, and also some women who had been healed of evil spirits and sicknesses: Mary who was called Magdalene, from whom seven demons had gone out, and Joanna the wife of Chuza, Herod's steward, and Susanna, and many others who were contributing to their support out of their private means" (Luke 8:1-3).

In this passage, Luke lumps the women right in with the famous twelve disciples. Even though on earth Christ possessed the very nature of God, His physical needs were just like ours…and He was homeless (Luke 9:58). So, because of His stature, His celebrity, it is easy to overlook the daily needs His ministry required. Likewise, it is easy to ignore the contributions that women made, especially when we consider all that happened in the scriptures, amidst the multiplicity of men serving Him.

Yet, Luke 8:1-3 declares there were some women who faithfully served His needs. Those women functioned with the same passion as men, and it was their enthusiasm that supplied Christ's physical needs: "It was by their gifts, no doubt, that Jesus and his company were enabled to live during the thirty or more months of the public ministry. He had given up, as had also his companions, his earthly occupation, and we know that he deliberately refrained from ever using his miraculous power to supply his daily wants."[36]

It is believed that Luke wrote his book to legitimize the testimony of Christ's preaching by drawing attention to those who had accompanied Him and had witnessed it. As theologian C.H. Talbert explained,

> Those who were 'with him' (vv. 1b-2) belong to two groups: (1) the Twelve and (2) the women. Both groups are designated by the evangelist [Luke] elsewhere as those who came with him from Galilee (23:49; 23:55; 24:10; Acts 1:11; 13:31). It appears to be Luke's intention to set the Twelve and the women alongside one another as guarantors of the facts of the Christ event.[37]

---

36. H. D. M. Spence-Jones (Ed.), *St. Luke* Vol. 1, (New York, NY: Funk & Wagnalls Company, 1909), 200. (Des Moines, WA: Biblesoft, Inc., 2015).

37. C. H. Talbert, *Reading Luke: A literary and theological commentary on the third Gospel* (Macon, GA: Smyth & Helwys Publishing, 2002), 93. (Des Moines, WA: Biblesoft, Inc., 2015).

The women and men with Christ witnessed the relentless attacks on Him, His poverty, and His earthly family's refusal to recognize His Messiahship. Still, Christ remained fervent about fulfilling His Father's agenda, and again, the agenda of God was the dominant concern He had. He did ministry all day, which included walking long distances on dusty, rocky roads (this is why foot washing was the custom of the day), facing the rejection of the Jewish leaders, and supporting the frailty of His disciples. That is why Luke 8:1 states, "He began going about from one city and village to another, proclaiming and preaching the kingdom of God."

The word "proclaiming" indicates that Jesus was shouting aloud. He was screaming, trying to compel the people, every day, all day, to accept the Good News God had provided. "Proclaim" literally means to stand on a rooftop and scream. Because His love of God was so compelling and because Jesus saw the needs of the people, the scripture says, "He saw a great multitude, and He felt compassion for them because they were like sheep without a shepherd; and He began to teach them many things" (Mark 6:34-35). When His love becomes our love, as per Matthew 22:36-40 and Philippians 2:1-5, then we are driven in the same way as the ladies of Luke 8:1-3. So let us examine what it was possibly like to follow Him.

Luke mentions Joanna, the wife of Chuza, a steward of Herod, as one of the women supporting Jesus by her own means. Joanna's husband served in upper management in Herod's kingdom; he was a person of prominence. This means Joanna was a woman of prominence, an aristocrat, yet she was faithful in helping fund Christ's ministry. She recognized and respected what Christ could do supernaturally and in turn was determined to help others, engaging directly in supporting Christ and serving Him. Commentator J. Calvin explained it this way:

Those matrons being wealthy and of high rank, it reflects higher commendation on their pious zeal, that they supply Christ's expenses out of their own property, and, not satisfied with so doing, leave the care of their household affairs, and choose to follow him, attended by reproach and many other inconveniences, through various and uncertain habitations, instead of living quietly...in their own houses.[38]

For Joanna, serving Christ in those days had to be hard work considering all she gave up to follow Him. Because of her husband's status, she most likely enjoyed a prosperous lifestyle. Yet, Joanna gave up that lifestyle to keep Christ's ministry functional. For example, think of where they might have slept. Remember Christ was homeless, having "had no place to lay His head" (Luke 9:58). If anything, a person usually has a place to sleep and some bread. Bread was viewed as a gift from God. Jesus had neither.

If that was the life that defined these women, imagine what it was like for a woman whose husband was a steward to the horrible Herod. I can only wonder how Joanna managed politics because her husband was never said to have been saved. Despite it all, she continuously served the physical needs of Christ, along with other women, like Mary Magdalene.

Mary Magdalene was totally devoted to Christ who had cast out seven demons from her. She was present at the crucifixion, determined to be an attentive witness. Though it was dark, and earthquakes were rattling the place, she stayed. Do you know how risky it was to be at the site of the crucifixion, a place swarming with Roman soldiers? Do you know how much riskier that was for a woman? There were probably no laws that would send a Roman soldier to jail for raping a Jewish woman. The Romans brutalized the Jews and were known

---

38. J. Calvin and W. Pringle, *Commentary on a Harmony of the Evangelists Matthew, Mark, and Luke* Vol. 2, (Bellingham, WA: Logos Bible Software, 2010), 100.

to have nailed as many as 500 to the cross in one day. Surely Mary Magdalene knew all that.

When Jesus died and was placed in the tomb, the Apostle Matthew wrote that "Mary Magdalene was there...sitting opposite the tomb" (Matthew 27:61). A few days later, at the resurrection, Mary Magdalene and other women went to the tomb with spices to anoint Christ's body—at sunrise (Mark 16:1-2). Now that's dedication! The other disciples, the men, were nowhere to be found.

Mary Madelene and Joanna were passionate about following Jesus. They gave money for the furtherance of His ministry. It was their love for Christ that energized and drove these women to sacrifice what-ever was needed for the purpose of progressing His ministry. Indeed, a curious fact that cannot be overlooked is how these women hailed from different strata of society but were made equal in their support of Jesus. One Bible scholar remarked, "It is an amazing thing to find Mary Magdalene, with the dark past, and Joanna, the lady of the court, in the one company."[39]

Many biblical scholars have commented on the fact that Jesus Christ elevated women in society. C.E. Arnold said, "Jesus shatters the societal conception of the inferiority of women, raising them to the status of disciples (unheard of in Judaism) and to a place of spiritual equality."[40] Bible scholar D.E. Bock goes on to say:

An exemplary faith is displayed by the woman who anoint Jesus and by those women who contribute to His ministry. Here the breadth of Jesus' ministry is emphasized as women, who were held in low esteem in the first century, are raised up as examples of faith. Here also in

---

39. *The Gospel of Luke.* (W. Barclay, Ed.). The Daily study Bible series (Philadelphia: The Westminster Press, 2000), 96. (Des Moines, WA: Biblesoft, Inc., 2015).

40. C. E. Arnold, *Zondervan Illustrated Bible*, 390. (Des Moines, WA: Biblesoft, Inc., 2015).

two scenes poor women, wealthy women, and women oppressed by Satan are all brought to equal honor by Jesus.[41]

Jesus Christ was definitely breaking taboos and stereotypes by elevating women to the rank of disciples, not to mention allowing them to accompany Him during his travels. Women of substance supporting Jesus financially was not that uncommon since such practices were accepted by teachers in Greco-Roman society. However, what was unusual was that the women traveled with him from town to town. Arnold also remarked, "What is uncommon is that these women travel with Jesus, a respected rabbi, and are treated as his disciples. Rabbis of this day did not have women disciples."[42]

Scripture attests to the fact that many, many women followed and supported Jesus. Luke 1:3 also mentions Susanna, whose name means "lily."[43] However, no light is shed on who she was, other than that she supported Christ from her own financial means. Still, it was common for women in the ancient Mediterranean world to serve as patrons and supporters of religious teachers and associations, though men were said to outnumber them because men had greater economic means, according to bible scholar C.S. Keener. Yet, to accompany Jesus and other men around the countryside…imagine the talk, the gossip!

…for these women to travel with the group would have been viewed as scandalous. Adult coeducation was unheard of, and that these women are learning Jesus' teaching as closely as his male disciples would surely bother some outsiders as well. Upper-class families had more mobility, but commoners would still talk, as they did when

41. D. L. Bock, "Luke," in *Holman concise Bible commentary*, ed. D. S. Dockery (Nashville, TN: Broadman & Holman Publishers, 1998), 453–455. (Des Moines, WA: Biblesoft, Inc., 2015).

42. Arnold, *Zondervan Illustrated Bible*, 391. (Des Moines, WA: Biblesoft, Inc., 2015).

43. Spence-Jones, *St. Luke*, 200). (Des Moines, WA: Biblesoft, Inc., 2015).

other teachers (such as Greek philosophers) were accused of having women among their followers.[44]

Furthermore, Luke 8:3 says that the women made contributions from their private means. Do you know what kind of contributions they made? It was not just money. It meant cooking for everyone in the traveling party. Now, consider the fact that there were no stoves like we have today, and they were moving around a lot, so no kitchen with an island and name-brand utensils. As for fuel, they were outside, using wood. (And remember, Martha once complained about Mary not helping prepare a meal, which probably meant killing an animal and preparing it from scratch.) Though most times the travelers only carried three pieces of clothing, those clothes still needed washing. Washing machines? Unheard of.

In reaction to a machine that had broken, I once heard a younger woman say to a senior woman, "Ah, it's like being back in the good old days." Puzzled, the senior woman looked at her and said, "What is good about the old days? There were no washing machines, dishwashers, electricity, and cars that could be started without needing to be cranked up." She said that compared to all she had in her kitchen now, the days past were not the "good old days." She told the woman, "I would have died for a kitchen like this with all the kids I was raising."

Mary Magdalene, Joanna, Susanna, and the many other women with Christ did not serve with the best equipment and under the best of circumstances. Yet, it did not matter because their grateful hearts were compelled by their love for Christ. Their service for Christ, whose life on earth was spent living below the poverty line, was of greater benefit to the completion of His ministry. Their loyalty to Christ carried such deep conviction.

---

44. Keener, *The IVP Bible background commentary.* (Des Moines, WA: Biblesoft, Inc., 2015).

Concerning love and loyalty, I am reminded of Anna in the temple. After her husband died, Anna served in the temple for possibly sixty years. Hers was a horrible job, cleaning guts and other animal parts from the instruments used in animal sacrifices. There were so many sacrifices that history notes how one side of Mount Zion would be covered with blood. Still, Anna faithfully executed her responsibilities while waiting for the day of redemption (when Christ entered the temple, and her prayers were answered). She faithfully executed her duties until she was eighty-four years old, all the while praying and hoping that she would see Jesus (Luke 2:36-38).

No one would probably think much of Anna doing that dirty job for so many years. It is not like anyone paid attention when she went through the temple courts holding the baby Jesus in her hands. However, God saw her heart and faithful labor. Along with Simeon, He honored her to experience baby Jesus and then included her story in the scriptures. While others may have considered her to be a devoted follower of God doing a menial job, God viewed her role as significant and therefore acknowledged her.

I am sure men like the high priests, Levites, scribes, Pharisees, and Rabbis received all the recognition, while Anna, to whom baby Jesus was entrusted, was the woman who did the nasty, temple-cleaning job. To her credit, Anna's spiritual maturity allowed her to see Jesus for who He was, unlike the aforementioned men who possessed a lot more knowledge. It is notable that they were so religious yet so blind, such that when Anna ran around the temple proclaiming the redemption of Israel, none of them ever joined her. These leaders served in a ritualistic manner in the hopes of fulfilling the law. Anna served faithfully, fulfilling the law with the hopes of seeing Christ. Her heart—not just her mind—was for God (1 Corinthians 8:1-2; 2 Peter 1:3-11).

Today, the appliances and amenities at our disposal can cause some to become self-serving. Many want to be "blessed in the city, blessed in the fields, blessed when they come and when they go." However, women like Joanna, Mary Magdalene, Susanna, and Anna were women who respected and followed Christ because they had a high sense of appreciation for who He was and for what He had done. Serving Christ with that kind of dedication can be a challenge, like it was for the church of Laodicea. In Revelation 3:15-18, the Laodiceans felt rich and powerful, but Christ viewed them as "wretched, miserable, poor, blind, and naked." The people who make a difference for Christ do not have to be rich or powerful or even males. They just need to be willing and obedient.

Shaped and compelled by their gratitude for all He did for them, the women fueled Jesus's very busy ministry schedule. They had no complaints, just a persistent commitment to witness the fulfillment of His Father's will. The impact that Christ, the son of the living God, was making on the public was obviously the story of the day. However, from a human standpoint, it was the women who kept His ministry supplied on a daily basis. These women may not be mentioned in the Hebrews 11 "Hall of Faith," but I am sure that on arriving in heaven, they will share His throne. They were unlike the church of Laodicea. They did not revel in their wealth. They sowed it in the service of Christ, not just by giving Him money but also by faithfully serving Him.

> But you have a few people in Sardis who have not soiled their garments; and they will walk with Me in white, for they are worthy. He who overcomes will thus be clothed in white garments; and I will not erase his name from the book of life, and I will confess his name before My Father and before His angels. He who has an ear, let him hear what the Spirit says to the churches. (Revelation 3:4-6, 18; 4:4; 7:9, 13).

Fast-forward to the twenty-first century. When one evaluates many of the churches that are active today, they are observed to be made up of more women than men. Yet, the steadfast accomplishments of women are often overlooked. Still, without them, the church today would not be as effective. The same was the case in Christ's earthly ministry. As stated, it was some of those women who remained at the site of the crucifixion, while, with the exception of John, Jesus's male disciples left Him.

I can attest to the impact of godly women in my own life. Who would have thought that a twelve-year-old boy from Guyana, South America would accomplish all that the Lord has blessed me to experience? If most of the people who are touched by the Living Word Fellowship Church and Power Walk Ministries had seen the twelve-year-old boy in Guyana, they would have probably never thought that the Lord would use him in the manner He has. It should be no surprise that it all started with my mother.

She would come into my room at night and teach me how to conduct devotions while removing my comic books from beneath my pillow. It was my mother who would get up every weekday morning, prepare lunch for my father, and then teach her eight children the scriptures. It was my mother who encouraged her husband to perform devotions with his children before church on Sunday mornings.

It was my mother who made sure that this twelve-year-old boy attended discipleship classes with her friend, Sister Clark, who faithfully came to disciple me even when no one else showed up. Sister Clark did that week after week, most times walking or riding her bicycle in the hot sun. When I stand to preach or teach, be it on radio, television, or through one of my books, no one sees those women. But it was the unseen female heroes who made all the difference in the life of a little boy from a small country in South America.

In the same way, many women, all of them unseen heroes, are mentioned in the New Testament as having made substantial contributions during the early days of the Church. A few are Dorcas, Lydia, Damaris, Priscilla, and Phoebe. Yet there are dozens whose names are not mentioned. These include the "…sisters who were in Lystra and Iconium" and who are mentioned in Acts 16. They sacrificed and served right alongside the Apostle Paul and others and should be considered soldiers and warriors fighting for the Christian faith. Many are honorably mentioned in Romans 16:8, 13, and 15.

Though short, the Luke 8:1-3 passage is a powerful one because it says a lot about women who were victorious in the spiritual war. Ignoring their own needs and desires, they sacrificed everything because they desired to see other people's lives changed like theirs had been. Similarly, the single-minded focus of the Macedonians of 2 Corinthians 8:1-6 is a source of inspiration. Women like Mary Magdalene, Joanna, and Susanna quietly blessed the ministry of Jesus Christ in a powerful manner. Perhaps, biblical commentator A.T. Roberson said it best: "Theirs was the first woman's missionary society for the support of missionaries of the Gospel. They had difficulties in their way, but they overcame these, so great was their gratitude and zeal."[45]

I began this chapter by relating a story about my encounter with men and women in uniform. I highlighted the sacrifices they made to uphold our freedoms. Their dedication, commitment to service, and love for their country enables us all to sleep comfortably in our beds while these men and women often sleep on the ground. We eat at dining tables while they struggle to keep sand out of their rations. Their sacrifices allow us to bathe in the comfort of our homes while they bathe when the opportunity presents itself. Here I am, an African-American

45. A.T. Robertson, *Word Pictures in the New Testament* (CCEL, 1930). (Des Moines, WA: Biblesoft, Inc., 2015).

man moving around freely, and yet, innumerable people have died to give me the freedoms I enjoy.

What dawned on me when I was rushing through the airport is that a covert war has been going on for thousands of years, and sometimes we ignore it. It is a war between God and Satan. This war has been going on from the time Satan was removed from heaven. The Enemy is constantly seeking to hinder God's agenda for mankind, and his entire focus is to kill, to steal, and to destroy (John 10:10; Revelation 12:10). That is why we are told to wear the armor of God so that we do not struggle against the call of flesh and blood. We struggle against an Enemy who is relentlessly seeking to devour us every day, as scripture explains: "Satan is a roaring lion seeking whom he may devour..." (Ephesians 6:10 -18; 1 Peter 5:8-11).

How could we ignore Jesus Christ fighting for us day and night at the right hand of God? During the time His body lay in the tomb, Christ even went to hell to declare to Satan's demons of Genesis 6:1-8 that they were doomed forever (1 Peter 3:18-20). He sits at the right hand of God, as our high priest, constantly interceding on our behalf (Hebrews 8:1-2), because Satan constantly seeks to impose a Job-like experience upon us (Revelation 12:10). Christ, like those soldiers in that busy airport, is constantly doing all He can to protect, empower, and mature us for a victorious Christian life.

All those who are Gentiles should be extremely appreciative because we were without hope of being included in the Kingdom of God (Ephesians 2:11-22). Now, we have the opportunity of the Holy Spirit pouring into us at the point of salvation (Titus 3:4-8) and have access to all spiritual blessings (Ephesians 1:3-4). We now have Christ as our mediator in heaven (Hebrews 8:1-2), our High Priest who intercedes for us. If we choose to live in complete commitment to the Word of God, we have angels to guard us (Hebrews 1:14). Paul puts it this way: "Therefore if you have been raised up with Christ, keep seeking the things above, where Christ is, seated at the right hand of God. Set your mind on the things above, not on the things that are on earth. For you have died and your life is hidden with Christ in God. When Christ, who is our life, is revealed, then you also will be revealed with Him in glory" (Colossians 3:1-4).

Even though we may not see our earthly circumstances changing, He can transform us from the inside—in such a way that the fruit of the Spirit can make us content and anxious for nothing amidst negative circumstances, as He works for our good (Philippians 2:13; 4:10-12; 4:4-9; Romans 8:28). So, no matter what we may face, we can do "all things through Christ who strengthens us" (Philippians 4:13). That is a short list of all Christ does for us daily because it does not include what happens when we choose to abide in Him; He places angels around us to preserve us from evil every day (Psalm 34:7; Hebrews 1:14). It is truly awe-inspiring. Like David was moved to ask in Psalm 8:4, when he thought of all that God did, "what is man that you are mindful of him?" When we arrive in heaven, we will learn of the innumerable acts our intercessor, Jesus Christ, performed on our behalf, acts that occur every moment of every day. And all of this occurred from a human standpoint, since Christ was fully human. And these unseen heroes played a significant role in assisting Christ each day of His earthly ministry. Thanks be to God!

All these eternal blessings are experienced because when the war began, these unsung heroes (not just His disciples) faithfully served Christ while on earth, so that He could execute His Father's will: "The Spirit of the Lord is upon Me, because He anointed Me to preach the gospel to the poor. He has sent Me to proclaim release to the captives, and recovery of sight to the blind, to set free those who are oppressed, to proclaim the favorable year of the Lord" (Luke 4:18-19). They served

Him so that He could faithfully, from a human standpoint, say on the cross, "It is finished." Most of these women stood there and watched Him at the height of the war, while His disciples (except John), were no-shows. Their faithfulness was determined by such a deep conviction that they remained until Christ gave up His Spirit—only to then come to the tomb to serve Him one last time, and that too at a point when no disciples were seeking Him.

These ladies may have never written a book in the Bible, but they stayed the course once they committed to engage in the battle Christ was charged to lead. This is why their names are recorded in scripture, and the men who served Christ did not forget to include them in the work of the Lord. These unsung female heroes enabled us to have the opportunity to experience "life and life abundantly" (John 10:10) because they willingly, faithfully served with seemingly no desire for accolades. They were passionately committed to the progress of the Gospel as their ultimate ambition. To God be the glory!

CHAPTER 7
Yes You Can!

*O*ver my many years in ministry, I have run into women whose past lifestyles and decisions might elicit a one-word response to the content of this book: IMPOSSIBLE! To such women, I say, "YOU CAN!" The Lord demonstrated that this is possible because of the kinds of women He chose to serve with Him in His earthly ministry.

I would have never thought Solomon would write three books in the Bible after acquiring 700 wives and 300 concubines in violation of Deuteronomy 17:17. Who could imagine that God would return David to being king of Israel after his offenses against Uriah and Bathsheba? Would anyone have picked Peter to be the keynote preacher at Pentecost? Imagine the Apostle Paul (the one who was born untimely, as per 1 Corinthians 15:8) who ended up writing half the New Testament after persecuting the church prior to his conversion. And then, there is Mary Magdalene.

Possessed by seven demons, she worked as a fortune teller, practicing witchcraft. A lucrative career for sure, yet did demons influence her life to the extent that she became a prostitute? Still, as stated in an earlier chapter, Mary was one of the women who eventually supported Jesus's ministry—the same Mary whom Jesus Christ, out of His love, kindness, and grace, delivered from a life of sin.

At Jesus Christ's resurrection, Mary was the recipient of special graces: the first to see the angels, the first to see the risen Christ alive, and the first to proclaim the Good News of His resurrection (John 20:11-18). "Christians today are also the recipients of special grace;

103

they too receive this new responsibility to carry the Gospel to the world (Matthew 28:16–20).[46]

There were at least three women who went to Jesus Christ's empty tomb to anoint His body with spices. Luke wrote that several other women were with them. It would be the last possible way to demonstrate their love for the Savior—and Mary Magdalene was among them (Luke 24:1). Mary had personally witnessed His crucifixion, seeing the earthquake at the cross, the darkness, the dead saints coming to life, and now His resurrection at the tomb...and she still wanted to know "Where did you lay Him?" (John 20:11-15).

In John's account of the resurrection, he focused on the actions of Mary Magdalene, even though he knew about the other women present with her. Mary's passionate actions totally impressed John, who himself had a special, loving relationship with Christ. Indeed, one would think the angels would have appeared to Peter or John, a relative of Jesus. However, the angels spoke to a formerly sinful, demon-possessed woman. Consider the dialogue between Mary Magdalene and the angels in John 20:11-18:

> But Mary was standing outside the tomb, weeping; and as she wept, she stooped to look into the tomb; and she saw two angels in white sitting, one at the head and one at the feet, where the body of Jesus had been lying. And they said to her, 'Woman why are you weeping?' She said to them, 'Because they have taken away my Lord and I do not know where they have laid him. And when she said this, she turned around and saw Jesus standing there and did not know that it was Jesus. And Jesus said to her, 'Woman why are you weeping? Whom are you seeking?' Supposing he was the gardener, she said to him, 'Sir if you have carried him away, tell me where you have laid

46. E. A. Blum, J. F. Walvoord and R. B. Zuck (Eds.) *The Bible Knowledge Commentary: An Exposition of the Scriptures* (Wheaton, IL: Victor Books, 1985). (Des Moines, WA: Biblesoft, Inc., 2015).

him, and I will take him away?' And Jesus said to her. 'Mary!' She turned to him and said in Hebrew, 'Rabboni!' which means teacher. Jesus said to her, 'Stop clinging to me. For I have not yet ascended to my Father; but go to my brethren and say to them, 'I ascend to My Father and to your Father, and to My God and to your God.' Mary Magdalene came and announced to the disciples, 'I have seen the Lord,' and he had said these things to her.'

To Mary, the angels were irrelevant; she had come for one person, Jesus Christ. Nothing else mattered. Please remember that it was still dark, and Mary was alone. That's passion, which is why I believe John focused his attention on Mary Magdalene, for even John himself had left the tomb by then.

Mary and the Great Commission

According to John 20:31, John wrote his account for one purpose: "... that ye might believe that Jesus is the Christ, the Son of God; and that believing ye might have life through his name."

Jesus did not engage in gender discrimination when it came to spreading news of His resurrection. As one commentator notes: "The fact that Jesus first entrusted the Great Commission to Mary is telling. For her new task or responsibility was the archetype eventually given to all believers, the entire Church: go and tell that Jesus has risen."[47] Imagine the shock the disciples experienced when Mary was the first to declare Christ's resurrection to them. "The significance of Jesus giving such a responsibility to Mary cannot be overemphasized. It was not a cultural norm in first-century Judaism for a woman's testimony to be accepted, let alone believed, which is perhaps why the disciples did not

---

47. Pfeiffer and Harrison, *The Wycliffe Bible Commentary*. (Des Moines, WA: Biblesoft, Inc., 2015).

believe Mary's report (Mark 16:11; Luke 24:11)."[48] Talk about shattering taboos. Nevertheless, as Bible commentator E.D. Radmacher explains, "Though it may be that Mary was formerly a woman of ill-repute, this did not keep Jesus from commissioning her to bring the gospel message to the apostles."[49]

Jesus Christ could have directed any of his male followers to carry the important message of His resurrection. (He did that later as per Mark 16:14-20.) However, our Lord was well-aware of how women were negatively viewed in the society of that time. Thus, He chose a woman, one of formerly ill repute, to deliver news of His resurrection to the disciples. No one can ever accuse Jesus Christ of being a misogynist!

A New Relationship Announced

When Mary finally recognized the person she was speaking to, her first reaction was to grab the resurrected Savior. (Perhaps, having lost Him once, she did not want to lose Him a second time.) Nonetheless, "Jesus said to her, 'Stop clinging to Me, for I have not yet ascended to the Father; but go to My brothers and say to them, "I am ascending to My Father and your Father, and My God and your God" ' " (John 20:17). There was an important reason why He said that.

Bible commentator Andrew Lincoln addresses why Jesus could not allow Mary to cling to Him: "…the desire to hold on to the bodily form of the risen Lord must be restrained. It impedes the realization of the new universal and abiding relationship with this Lord."[50]

The Wycliffe Bible Commentary explains that Christ's words to

48. Arnold, *Zondervan Illustrated Bible,* 188 (Des Moines, WA: Biblesoft, Inc., 2015).

49. Radmacher, Allen and House, *Nelson's New Illustrated Bible Commentary.* (Des Moines, WA: Biblesoft, Inc., 2015).

50. A. T. Lincoln, *The Gospel According to Saint John* (London: Continuum, 2005), 493–494. (Des Moines, WA: Biblesoft, Inc., 2015).

Mary meant "a new relationship, new relatives, and a new responsibility. Mary needed to be taught that the Lord was not with her on the basis of the old relationship. He was already glorified. He belonged now to the heavenly realm, even though he was willing to tarry for a time to meet with his friends."[51]

Theologian Edwin A. Blum also elaborates on the meaning behind Jesus' admonition to Mary. In effect, Jesus said:

> 'This (the physical contact) is not My real presence for the church. A *new relationship* will begin with My Ascension and the gift of the Holy Spirit to the church.' Jesus then explained the fact of the *new relatives*. He called His disciples His brothers. Earlier He had said they were friends: 'I no longer call you servants...instead, I have called you friends' (John 15:15). Believers in Jesus become a part of Jesus' family with God as their Father.' (Heb. 2:11–12; Rom. 8:15–17, 29; Gal. 3:26)[52]

Thus, having been the first to be entrusted with spreading the news of His resurrection, Mary was also the first to receive news about the new relationship between the Son of God and those who believe in Him.

Love, Mary's Motivation

In John's description of events, he said Mary was standing outside the tomb and "weeping." John did not use the Greek word for "crying." The Greek word for "weeping" means *noise*. Mary Magdalene was loud; her weeping permeated the garden (John 20:11).

That Mary loved Jesus was an incontestable fact, but there were

---

51. Pfeiffer and Harrison, *The Wycliffe Bible Commentary*. (Des Moines, WA: Biblesoft, Inc., 2015).

52. Blum, Walvoord and Zuck, *The Bible Knowledge Commentary*. (Des Moines, WA: Biblesoft, Inc., 2015).

other reasons she may have wept so forcefully. Discovering that His body was missing must have been an overwhelming surprise. Theologian C.S. Keener explains as follows:

> Jewish culture was serious about expressing rather than repressing grief. Jewish people took the first seven days of mourning so seriously that mourners could not wash, work, have intercourse or even study the law.... That the body is missing and thus people are prevented from bestowing final acts of love would be regarded as intolerably tragic; even tomb robbers usually left the body behind.... Mary weeps, not because Jesus has died, but because his body has vanished; abuse of the dead was considered an abhorrent offense.[53]

On various news channels, we sometimes see people in Eastern cultures screaming and openly grieving at funerals. Similarly, Mary lost it when she discovered Jesus's body had gone missing. First, the pain of seeing Him crucified, and then the pain of His body disappearing—it was too much. Perhaps she thought, "My last chance to demonstrate my love, and someone steals His body. Really?"

Mary loved Christ so much that she saw no point in leaving the tomb until someone explained where they had taken Him. From her actions, it is clear that Mary did not simply go to the tomb to anoint His body with spices; she also intended to spend just one last moment with Him (John 20:1; Luke 24:1). Further, Mary Magdalene would not leave the tomb. The soldiers, who were seasoned warriors, left. The ladies returned home, but Mary stayed, even though it was dark.

That is what I love about the Apostle John's narrative. Even though Mary was overwhelmed with sorrow, she remained at the tomb because the only person who could direct her life was not there. So where would she go? Jesus honors the kind of passionate desire that seeks Him first

---

53. Keener, *The IVP Bible Background Commentary*. (Des Moines, WA: Biblesoft, Inc., 2015).

(Luke 12:31-32). No wonder, then, that Jesus appeared to Mary, and she knew His voice (John 10:14, 27).

It should not be surprising that it was Mary who showed up after the resurrection, looking for Jesus' body. After all, she had witnessed his battered, scarred body staggering along the road to Calvary. She had seen him being nailed to the cross. She had stood and watched as Jesus Christ gave up the ghost, and she was there when they removed His limp body from the cross and laid it in a tomb (John 19:25; Luke 23:49, 55-56). Despite all the evidence that Christ was dead, Mary was only interested in serving Jesus who had rescued her from the clutches of Satan. After her initial arrival, Mary soon left to retrieve the disciples. Some did come to the tomb on their own, but they eventually left. Not Mary. She went inside the tomb to examine it for herself.

Perhaps, John's narrative highlights why Christ took the time to openly engage His disciples in the Luke 7:36-50 incident. In that passage, an unknown "sinful woman" with an alabaster jar of perfume wept over Jesus's feet, wiped them with her hair, and then anointed them with the perfume. Later in the same passage, Jesus tells a story about a debtor who had been forgiven a large debt, and afterward, he forgives the woman her sins. Also in the Luke 7 passage, Jesus compares the forgiven woman with the Pharisees who, because of their holy status, gave Him no respect—quite unlike the forgiven woman.

For a moment, consider who killed Jesus Christ as opposed to who wept at His tomb. Think of where His disciples were at His crucifixion and His burial as opposed to who was found weeping at the tomb. Then consider to whom Christ first appeared and who he instructed to go and tell His disciples the good news of His resurrection. In every case—it was Mary Magdalene.

Grace Prompts Absolute Surrender

One would think Mary would be the last person Jesus Christ would address after His resurrection, not the first. The woman who had once been possessed by seven demons was not going to be an apostle, nor would she sit in heaven as one of the rulers of the twelve tribes of Israel. So why talk to Mary Magdalene first? Because she treasured grace. Jesus chose the person who demonstrated a heart for him—not a mind, but a heart.

Being saved is to bring heaven to earth. Or as the Apostle Paul would say in Galatians 2:20, "…it is no longer I who live, but Christ lives in me…" Jesus Christ died to become our friend and to provide us abundant life (John 15:13; John 10:10). Furthermore, our Lord characterizes believers as "the salt of the earth" and "the light of the world," so our purpose for being saved now is to serve as salt and light to a dying world (Matthew 5:13-16).

Mary treasured Jesus Christ's transforming power; her devotion to Him changed her life. That is why she treasured her relationship with Him. She did not just attend to Christ when He was speaking in her vicinity. She "no longer lived" with any concerns about her life goals; it was all about Christ and His ministry. In John 20:11, her dedication became even more evident.

Mary Magdalene knew what His transformation had done for her. So, she appreciated His grace, and Christ's love moved Mary to love Him unquestionably. Mary understood and surely recalled that at one time she had been possessed by seven demons and had been doomed to hell. She could never have entered the temple; her sins could never have been forgiven. There was no place she could have gone where people would not have ostracized her. For even though she was a Jew, the fact that she had been possessed by seven demons meant only those who trusted in witchcraft would come near her.

It is not a person's past that is the issue at hand (because Christ takes care of that completely). It is a person's decisions in the present that determine how powerful and effective their future will be. When our passion for Christ dominates our lives, we become laser-focused like Mary Magdalene.

Mary's love for Christ so transformed her life that it prompted full surrender in the present, making her past irrelevant. However, even though Mary's love for Christ erased her past, she stood hopelessly lost at the tomb, asking, "Where have you laid Him?" Even when Christ began to speak to her, she demonstrated no expectation that He would be living and spoke to Him as if He was the gardener. This led Christ to ask, "Woman why are you weeping." In other words, "Why are you putting so much energy into mourning rather than rejoicing?"

Does Christ's grace create that kind of appreciation and love in us toward Him? Every day, every moment of the day, do we want to see Him and hear from Him? Do we come to the scriptures to hear what he has to say and are so passionate toward Him that He dominates how we walk with Him?

A little rain or bad weather keeps us from church, but not from work. A bad experience with someone at church runs us out the door, but a similar encounter does not keep us away from difficult people at work where we earn money. We sometimes assign more love and time to animals than we do to God.

In Wisconsin, the temperatures can sometimes drop below 20 °F or 40 °F. When I was there, I thought to myself, "Even the birds know to fly south." Yet in that freezing cold, people get up on Sunday mornings and not merely go to an open stadium but have tailgate parties before football games. Some even remove their shirts during the game, cheering on the football team because they scored a touchdown. And some people might consider suicide if their team did not make it to the Superbowl, (or managed to make it and lost). Just imagine: all that fervor for a football team! Still, that's passion. When will Jesus mean that much to us?

We have heard sermons about how we are forgiven by the blood of Jesus and how our sins are removed from us as far as the east is from the west. We have heard how He washed us as white as snow, how we are brand-new creations, and old things have passed away (2 Corinthians 5:17). We have read how Paul says, "For I am convinced that neither death, nor life, nor angels, nor principalities, nor things present, nor things to come, nor powers, nor height, nor depth, nor any other created thing, will be able to separate us from the love of God, which is in Christ Jesus our Lord" and how, as a result, "in all these things we overwhelmingly conquer through Him who loved us" (Romans 8:38-39; Romans 8:8:17). That is why we conclude that we can do "all things through Christ who strengthens us" (Philippians 4:13). Nevertheless, though we may have a passion for Him, are excited about Him, and may feel that we love Him, do we honestly walk away believing what Christ says?

We can have intimate knowledge of ecclesiology, pneumatology, and biblical doctrines from the Bible, but do we really believe it when it contradicts what we think? Do we believe the Word of God with such a deep conviction that if we do not know what to do, we still wait on the Lord? As promised in Isaiah 40:31, "Yet those who wait for the Lord will gain new strength; they will mount up with wings like eagles, they will run and not get tired, they will walk and not become weary."

We must not merely hear the Lord's message. We must also trust Him when the circumstances make His message seem unbelievable. Our overwhelming circumstances and past experiences may make us feel lost, even hopeless. Still, believe God's Word because He promises to reward faith (Hebrews 11:6). The only fight we have in this life is whether we will keep the faith or not, especially when circumstances seem overwhelming (1 Timothy 6:12), and our pasts seem unforgivable.

Eve vs. Mary Magdalene

A contrast between Eve and Mary Magdalene highlights the importance of a woman's choices—and the consequences.

Eve was a woman who decided not to listen to the Word of God but to Satan in the form of a snake. Further, Eve chose the Tree of the Knowledge of Good and Evil over the Tree of Life. By contrast, Mary Magdalene, who suffered the sinful effects of Eve's decision, remained with the Tree of Life, Jesus Christ. And because of her persistence, which is a true display of faith, Jesus Christ honored Mary, despite her past, and spoke to her first after His resurrection. Thus, it was Mary who delivered to men, Jesus's disciples, the Good News of the Gospel: He has risen! While common sense first won in the Garden of Eden, which led to a message of death through Adam (Romans 5:12-17), Mary's faith now travels as a message of life through Jesus Christ.

So today, no longer can women be blamed for sin entering the world (Romans 5:12-13). Now women are redeemed from this incorrect message that had plagued them for centuries. Christ absolved women of their role in what took place in the Garden of Eden in Genesis 3.

The Comprehensive Nature of Grace

God's grace is so comprehensive, so generous and unearned, that nothing can be compared to it. When God's grace is appreciated responsibly (Romans 6:1-2), there is no way it would not transform a person's life. Once transformed, everything old becomes new (2 Corinthians 5:17). (A meaningful discipleship process makes that a reality.) Mary's attitude, focus, and unprecedented approach to seeking Christ allowed Him to rectify a wrong and re-elevate her life to its full potential.

We see the same happening with the woman who had been bleeding for the past twelve years in Mark 5:25-34. Remember, hers was such a bad case that her blood flowed down the unpaved roads. The woman could not go to the temple to be cleansed due to her predicament. Thus, those around the woman had concluded that her sins were many. That is why when the crowd was pressing around Jesus, she could make her way to Him because no one wanted to be touched by her. Yet, before those very people in Mark 5:34, Christ called her "daughter," and said, "your faith has made you well; go in peace and be healed of your affliction" (not your "sin" or "sickness," but your "affliction"). From that point forward, she was fully reinstated to her former status in her village.

Similarly, Jesus Christ, the Son of the living God, not only bestowed His grace upon Mary Magdalene but also enabled her to openly walk with Him, to be identified with Him, to be a part of His ministry—which could have hurt His ministry's reputation, considering her background. Yet, Christ loved Mary more than His own reputation.

Maybe that is why Paul put it this way: "And He has said to me, 'My grace is sufficient for you, for power is perfected in weakness. Most gladly, therefore, I will rather boast about my weaknesses, so that the power of Christ may dwell in me' " (2 Corinthians 12:9). That is why grace must be transforming.

So appreciative was Mary of all that Christ had done that she completely surrendered her life to Him. She was not merely focused on going to heaven. No, Mary's response to Jesus's blessing was absolute devotion to Him, and thus her life answers questions posed in Romans 6:1: "What shall we say then? Are we to continue in sin so that grace may increase?" Indeed, Mary's response to Christ should be an example to us all.

Nothing is impossible with God (Luke 2:37). Our past does not matter. What matters most is our willingness to accept God's grace, to become so appreciative that our entire focus mimics the disposition, devotion, passion, and persistent drive to seek Christ that was modeled by Mary Magdalene. When that is accomplished, we become strong despite our weaknesses (2 Corinthians 12:7-10).

This is what women who were Biblical heroes exemplified for us. Most of them did not come from high positions or status. It was their faith that paved the way. They were not patriarchs, nor biblical writers of scripture. They were simply like Ruth who positioned herself to help a woman named Naomi, a woman destined to a life of poverty and death (Ruth 1:16). They were like Dorcas who simply wanted to help widows (Acts 9:36-42), or Anna who chose to faithfully serve in the temple, praying and hoping to see the Messiah, the redemption of Israel (Luke 2:36-38). One must not forget Deborah who merely wanted to adjudicate the matters of the people against the Word of God (Judges 4). She did so faithfully, expeditiously, and with integrity, such that God took notice and spoke to her instead of to Barak, who obviously would not have listened attentively enough to lead His people to victory over their oppressor (Judges 4:5).

Great leaders do not have to occupy places of honor or key positions in government or the church. Great leaders see a need, and because of their commitment to first be led by God, they make a difference through the power of God in them (Ephesians 1:3-4). They take initiative, not seeking the praise of men (Matthew 25:34-30); they love the Lord's people (John 13:34-35) and become bondslaves for Him (John 20:11-18). We all are provided with a spiritual gift (1 Peter 4:10). It is imperative that we employ it for God's glory and honor. The past has been wiped clean (Psalm 103:12; Psalm 25:1-22). It is what we do in the present that determines how the transformative power of God works in and through us. Paul, who performed so many violent acts against the church, puts it this way:

> Not that I have already obtained it, or have already become perfect, but I press on in order that I may lay hold of that for which also I was laid hold of by Christ Jesus. Brethren, I do not regard myself as having laid hold of it yet; but one thing I do: forgetting what lies behind and reaching forward to what lies ahead, I press on toward the goal for the prize of the upward call of God in Christ Jesus. Let us therefore, as many as are perfect, have this attitude; and if in anything you have a different attitude, God will reveal that also to you; however, let us keep living by that same standard to which we have attained (Philippians 3:12-16).

The mindset like the one above leads to eternal blessings and the understanding: "For to me, to live is Christ and to die is gain" (Philippians 1:21).

We hope the Biblical accounts of the women highlighted in this book have added to your understanding of just how much God values people whose hearts are completely His (2 Chronicles 16:9). For certain, there are many more women in the Bible who are considered *sheroes* of the faith, some of whom are even mentioned in Hebrews 11. Thus, those inclined to limit or discount the contributions of women in the Kingdom plan of God are misinformed. For when one reads chapters two and three of Revelation, overcomers are promised rewards—and there's no suggestion that those rewards are doled out based on gender. When believers of this Church Age stand before our Lord at the Judgment Seat of Jesus Christ, rest assured, He will NOT relegate women to the back of the line (2 Corinthians 5:10; Romans 14:12; 1 Corinthians 3:13-14).

Made in the USA
Columbia, SC
09 November 2024

45819878R00065